gta edition 3

FLOWCHARTING

FROM ABSTRACTIONISM TO ALGORITHMICS IN ART AND ARCHITECTURE

MATTHEW ALLEN

PROLOGUE	07
FROM *CIRCLE* TO *DATA*: AVANT-GARDE ROUTINES	15
STRUCTURALISM: THE FORM OF LANGUAGE	57
STRUCTURALIST ACTIVITY IN *FORM*	73
MOTIVATING THE ALGORITHM	101
THE FLOWCHART AS ALGORITHMIC TECHNIQUE	111
PROGRAMMING ARCHITECTURE	135
ANNEX	145
Bibliography	146
Image Credits	154
Acknowledgments	155

PROLOGUE

The assembly line has long been a central conceptual icon of modernity: Render a process in mechanistic terms and it can surely be implemented by a machine. In this line of thinking, the rewards of progress follow in the footsteps of step-by-step rationality. Unencumbered by complicated human values, there is a certain freedom and joy to the logic of the assembly line, and in moments of grandiosity it can seem as if applying this logic at the scale of the globe would solve the trickiest problems humanity currently faces. Karl Marx must have been feeling this optimism when he observed that, in the modern world, "all that's solid melts into air"—as if the atmosphere of our times could be a transparent and even liberatory medium once it has been clarified by the ruthless rationality of economics. But there is a flaw in this reasoning: A real assembly line is not a matter of tidy logic, but a sprawling material system plugged into all manner of equipment, infrastructure, and bureaucracy that requires an array of techniques for flow management and design.

This essay tells a story of how architecture came to imagine itself as a discipline that contends fundamentally with flows. As the title suggests, a type of diagram developed initially in the fields of management science and computer programming—the flowchart—played an essential epistemological role. Confronted with the bewildering consequences of nineteenth-century industrialization, architects found themselves lacking necessary concepts and techniques. Flowcharts rendered certain kinds of flows understandable to architects. Although the flowchart was imported, the process of importation was motivated from within by a complicated set of disciplinary priorities that were themselves developed in conjunction with other fields, notably modern art. A decades-long, interdisciplinary exchange of ideas and methods ensued, resulting in a re-tooled theory of architecture by the middle of the last century.

It was a messy process. Perhaps the keenest observer of modern architecture as it crossed the channel from mainland Europe into England a hundred year ago, the theorist and critic John Summerson was alert to slippages between ideals and material practices in the design of built environments. Assessing the movement in retrospect at midcentury, Summerson saw modernist architectural theory itself as an unappealing outflow: He described the verbiage generated by revered figures like Le Corbusier and Bruno Zevi as "theoretical effluent," evoking the image of a sewage treatment plant for architectural theory.[1] Even as he faced this nauseous stew of classicism, futurism, grandiose moralizing, and dry technicalities, mainstream consensus found it expedient to declare modernism "history," dump the waste, and attempt to move on.[2]

Despite wishful thinking, the situation in which architecture finds itself has hardly changed: The processes and practices of architecture tend to overflow the neat bracketing of theory. Summerson illustrated the architect's role in a diagram depicting the circulation of money in the building industry (fig. 1). It shows the architect at the interface between his staff, waiting eagerly to design, and the client, gatekeeper to a vault stuffed with cash. The drawing set he passionately presents serves as a spigot for the flow of capital. In Summerson's accompanying text (written for a national newsmagazine, *The Listener*), he explains that 80 percent of this treasure is destined to be distributed in the form of wages to laborers, who are shown at the bottom of the diagram with their pickaxes, steam shovels, and welding torches. Summerson notes that this flow is an issue of supreme importance because, viewed in its fullest, the building industry sprawls outward in complicated supply chains across the countryside: "We need to realize the huge extent

---

[1] John Summerson, "The Case for a Theory of Modern Architecture," *Journal of the Royal Institute of British Architects* 64, no. 8 (June 1957): 307–10, here 309.

[2] Charles Jencks's declaration that the death of modern architecture occurred in 1972 was among the most iconic moments in this process. Charles Jencks, *The Language of Post-Modern Architecture* (New York: Rizzoli, 1977).

of the industrial hinterland which feeds the industry with material and equipment."[3]

This situation posed a problem for those who considered themselves to be the avant-garde of modernism—the disciplinary deciders, the intellectual tastemakers. Given the torrential flow of capital directed by the plans they draw, *what should they draw?* Given architects' significant control over the built environment, *what should that environment be like?* If there was a single central idea of modernism, it was that these questions should not be left to tradition—they would have to come up with their own answers to fit current conditions.

Soon after beginning his career as an architect, Summerson entered into the roiling midst of these debates, and his writing from the 1930s through the 1960s is a singularly insightful guide to the problems brewing in modern architecture during this period. After graduating from The Bartlett Faculty of the Built Environment at University College London, Summerson worked as an architect and taught in Edinburgh. In a few years he moved back to London to work for the Modern Architecture Research Group, a think tank founded by a group of modernist architects, as a researcher, organizer, writer, curator, and lobbyist for the cause of modernism. From this vantage point Summerson witnessed the arrival of the International Style and the work of its most prominent representative, the Swiss French architect Le Corbusier. He saw the frenzied adulation (his reporting at times clung with a hint of irony on Le Corbusier's every word), and he saw its waning importance as the fashion faded.[4] But Summerson also noticed that architecture was undergoing a lasting shift. The architect was no longer "a scholar and a gentleman ... with clients in the aristocracy, the City and the

---

3 John Summerson, "Building Boom – I," *The Listener* 468 (December 1937): 1418–20, here 1418.

4 John Summerson, "Introduction," in *Modern Architecture in Britain*, ed. Trevor Dannatt (London: Batsford, 1959), 11–28, here 15.

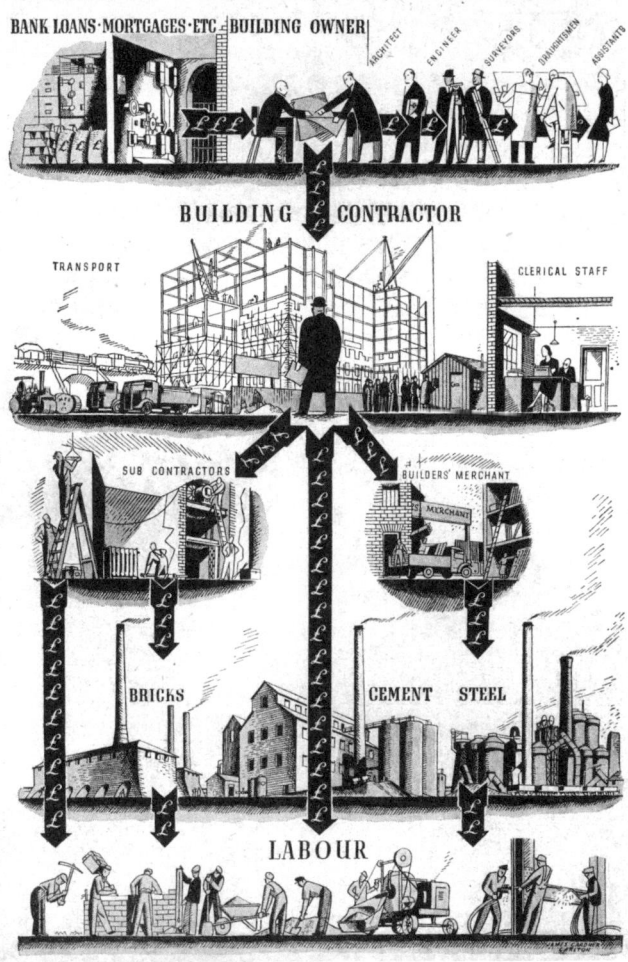

1   John Summerson, *Circulation of Money in the Building Industry*, 1937

Church."[5] Architects were now designing housing, hospitals, and schools. After the Second World War, reconstruction pressures shifted the discipline dramatically towards the practical.[6] For guidance in this new professional climate, Summerson looked to the massive projects recently erected by the Tennessee Valley Authority, and he saw a type of architecture agnostic to traditional aesthetics, leaving engineers in charge.[7] This created a precarious situation for architects: "On large-scale work today, [the architect] is obliged to delegate more and more to specialists, so that his basic function is coming to be that of planner and general adviser to the building owner."[8] Following the American trend, small firms were giving way to behemoths—the architecture department of the London County Council (that is, London's municipal government) was among the largest architectural offices in the world—but the persona of the architect had not kept up with the times.[9] Even as new registration laws defined the architect legally "not as an exponent of styles but as a technician with a special function and special obligations towards the public," the internal view still saw the architect as a "poet innovator."[10]

For Summerson, resolving this tension between practices and personas would require updating architectural theory. In a series of essays and lectures, Summerson traced dominant theories of modern architecture back through the French rationalist tradition, and he found that Le Corbusier

---

5 John Summerson, "Bread & Butter and Architecture," *Horizon* vi (October 1942): 233–43, here 233.

6 See Summerson, "Introduction."

7 John Summerson, "TVA: Adventure in Planning," *The Listener* 774 (November 1943): 558.

8 Summerson, "Building Boom," 1419.

9 On the American trend, see Jay Wickersham, "Learning from Burnham: The Origins of American Architectural Practice," *Harvard Design Magazine* 32 (2010): 18–27; for more on architects in the London County Council, see Elain Harwood, "London County Council Architects," in *Oxford Dictionary of National Biography* (Oxford: Oxford University Press, 2009), https://doi.org/10.1093/ref:odnb/97268.

10 John Summerson, "Architecture: A Changing Profession," *The Listener* 536 (April 1939): 830–32, here 831; Summerson, "Bread & Butter," 233.

was more indebted to Dominique Perrault, Marc-Antoine Laugier, and Eugène Viollet-le-Duc than the engineers he delighted in citing.[11] At the core of this lineage was an essentially classical language of form: "the play of volumes, disposed with masterly and superb exactitude beneath the light," as Le Corbusier famously put it.[12] By contrast, identifiably modernist theories like those of Bruno Zevi and László Moholy-Nagy pointed in a different direction, to the "organic," the "biological," and the "social." Although Summerson found these theories far from coherent (recall his comment about modernist theoretical "effluent"), at their base was something quite different from *form*: They always referred to "some rhythmically repetitive pattern—whether it is a manufacturing process, the curriculum of a school, the domestic routine of a house, or simply the sense of repeated movement in a circulation system."[13] Summerson incisively observed that modern architecture is all about *program*. He delivered his conclusive statement on the matter in 1963: "The modern school holds to the programme as the source of unity; the conception of a building must arise from within the programme; the programme itself must be the architect's medium, just as much as the materials with which he builds."[14] Such a statement did not resolve the problem, however, but merely identified it clearly: Architects would still need to find the "missing architectural language" for working with rhythmically repetitive patterns.

Architects developed a language for conceptualizing and designing flows over the course of several decades. By the 1960s, the flowchart had become a key instrument for planning sequences of actions and effects (that is, algorithms) in a way that could be implemented on an abstract machine (a building, in this view, is one such machine). This

---

11 Summerson, "Case for a Theory," 308.
12 Le Corbusier quoted in John Summerson, *The Classical Language of Architecture* (London: Methuen & Co, 1963), 41–42.
13 Summerson, "Case for a Theory," 309.
14 Summerson, "Introduction," 11.

language of flowcharting was developed initially in scientific management and what would later be called computer science, and a crucial detour through artistic movements grappling with the legacy of constructivism rendered the language in an idiom understandable to architects. None of this occurred smoothly. The conceptual disjunctions between these fields played an important role in motivating the use of flowcharts and algorithms; translating between fields required difficult and rewarding intellectual labor. Could paintings be created on something like an assembly line? Could a poem be reimagined as a sequence of effects? Could typologically similar buildings be generated using a shared algorithm?

As they were doing a century ago, architects are now trying to figure out what techniques their discipline has for working with systemic problems such as the "rhythmically repetitive patterns" of humanity pumping carbon into the atmosphere. More than ever the world is made up of large socio-technical systems, in the parlance of science and technology studies. The building industry is one such system, and architects should again ask themselves how flows of capital can be re-directed to create better built environments. Note that these systems are not usually designed—instead, they accrete over time—and so the tendency is to fall back on the familiar realm of form and traditional modes of design. Thus the question arises again: How can architects reconceptualize their discipline in terms of the language of flows?

FROM *CIRCLE* TO *DATA*: AVANT-GARDE ROUTINES

The twenty years between Summerson's optimistic "Building Boom" essay of 1937 and the soul-searching of his 1957 retrospective on modernist theory was a chasm of war, economic turmoil, and reconstruction pressures that left architects and artists struggling to pick up the threads of earlier agendas. A collection that appeared in 1968—*Data: Directions in Art, Theory and Aesthetics*—encapsulates how British artists navigated this interregnum while building the case for their own work as the next step in the development of modern art. The editor of *Data* enthused that it was "the first English publication of its kind since *Circle*," and it is to this most iconic publication of British modernism that we now turn for context.[15]

The period around 1960 was the shining moment for *Circle*.[16] The year the volume came out, 1937, was decidedly not an opportune moment for immediate impact. Britain would declare war two years later, and the interest being cultivated in "constructive art" would fall by the wayside. *Circle* was all but forgotten for over a decade.[17] Two decades later, however, the artists and architects whose work was published in *Circle* were established figures. One of its editors, the architect Leslie Martin, was head of the architecture school at the University of Cambridge, and his students would look

---

15 Anthony Hill, "Editor's Forward," in *Data: Directions in Art, Theory and Aesthetics*, ed. Anthony Hill (London: Faber & Faber, 1968), 5–6, here 5–6. This essay focuses on three idiosyncratic collections: *Data*, *Circle*, and *Form*. Only *Data* was published as a periodical, but all three sprang from the ethos of the "little magazine," which is a form that is invaluable to the historian in the way it tends to capture a slice of work within an artistic community in its bewildering complexity. For more on little magazines, see Beatriz Colomina, *Clip, Stamp, Fold: The Radical Architecture of Little Magazines, 196X to 197X* (Barcelona: Actar, 2011).

16 Leslie Martin, Ben Nicholson, and Naum Gabo, eds., *Circle: International Survey of Constructive Art* (London: Faber & Faber, 1937).

17 *Circle* "had little impact at the time; it was not until around 1950 that the ideas of Constructivism were to have wider recognition in England." George Rickey, *Constructivism: Origins and Evolution* (New York: Braziller, 1995), 51. See also Leslie Martin, "Introduction," in *Circle: Constructive Art in Britain 1934–40*, ed. Jeremy Lewison (Lavenham: Lavenham Press, 1982), 5–6.

upon *Circle* as a manifesto and a benchmark against which postwar accomplishments should be measured.[18]

It is ironic that a publication so suffused with anonymity would come to be seen as a definitive statement. *Circle* was conceived as a periodical, and it does vaguely resemble previous little magazines in its somewhat eclectic and mostly avant-garde content.[19] Its layout, however, is tidy and sparse, even serene—a far cry from the frenetic jumble of avant-garde magazines of the 1920s, such as *G: Material zur elementaren Gestaltung* (Material for elementary construction) in Berlin and *ABC: Beiträge zum Bauen* (Contributions to building) in Zurich / Basel. While these precedents offered dense combinations of subjects and genres to undermine distinctions between writing, editing, illustration, layout, typography, and printing, *Circle* reinstates neat divisions between artistic genres.[20] Set in Helvetica typeface throughout, with images typically occupying their own pages and surrounded by plenty of white space, *Circle* embodies the advice offered by the modernist typographer Jan Tschichold in one of its articles: "Clear presentation" and "immaculate technique" create "the contemporary feeling of space" through graphic design.[21]

Circle's impulse toward anonymity continued at the editorial level. There is little explicitly polemical writing to be found in the volume, and the theme of unity is zealously

---

18 See, e.g., Anthony Hill, "Constructivism: The European Phenomenon," *Studio International* 171, no. 876 (April 1966): 140–47.

19 Martin, "Introduction," 5.

20 See Monoskop, "Avant-Garde and Modernist Magazines," August 2014, http://monoskop.org/Avant-garde_and_modernist_magazines.

21 Jan Tschichold, "The New Typography," in *Circle: International Survey of Constructive Art*, ed. Leslie Martin, Ben Nicholson, and Naum Gabo (London: Faber & Faber, 1937), 249–55. We are reminded that *Circle* stands halfway between Tschichold's Bauhaus modernist manifesto—*New Typography* (1928)—and his later return to the rules of classical typography in his redesign of Penguin's paperbacks (1947). *Circle* likewise feels caught between the radical and the reactionary. *Circle*'s publisher, Faber & Faber, was in a similar moment of transition. Having been founded in 1929, it was well on its way to becoming the established press of British modernism by 1937, with figures such as T. S. Eliot in its catalog.

maintained on every page. Indeed, a guiding fiction of *Circle* is that no editorial direction was involved at all. The opening editorial statement, which is unsigned, declares to have found "a new cultural unity" and to be presenting ideas that have "grown spontaneously" in "the mind of society."[22] The content of the publication, running to almost three hundred pages, alternates between sections of images and sections of de-contextualized artist statements. Contrary to the cherished avant-gardist technique of juxtaposing contradictory content, *Circle* is parsed under the most banal of headings: Painting, Sculpture, Architecture, and Art and Life (the last of which was a trope of interwar modernism[23]).

All this was a wishful ruse. The editors of *Circle* were in fact stars nurturing ascent to fame. Martin was teaching at the University of Hull, where he had invited many of the architects who contributed to *Circle* as guest speakers—Maxwell Fry, Marcel Breuer, László Moholy-Nagy—thereby setting himself up as a nodal point of international modernist culture.[24] Martin was at the same time cultivating a private practice with Sadie Speight based on residential commissions for friends in the art world.[25] Another of *Circle*'s editors, Ben Nicholson, was a British painter who had been singled out alongside Piet Mondrian as a main representatives of geometrical abstraction by Alfred Barr, the director of the Museum of Modern Art in New York (fig. 2).[26] The third editor was Naum Gabo, an émigée sculptor and the most famous of the trio. If there was a single reason for the publication of *Circle*, it

22 Martin, Nicholson, and Gabo, *Circle*, v.
23 See, e.g., Jacques Rancière, *Aisthesis: Scenes from the Aesthetic Regime of Art* (New York: Verso, 2011).
24 Peter Carolin, "Martin, Sir (John) Leslie," in *Oxford Dictionary of National Biography* (Oxford: Oxford University Press, 2013), https://doi.org/10.1093/ref:odnb/74528.
25 Adam Sharr, *Demolishing Whitehall: Leslie Martin, Harold Wilson and the Architecture of White Heat* (Farnham, UK: Ashgate, 2013), 153.
26 Alfred H. Barr, *Cubism and Abstract Art; Painting, Sculpture, Constructions, Photography, Architecture, Industrial Art, Theatre, Films, Posters, Typography* (New York: Museum of Modern Art, 1936); Christopher Green and Barnaby Wright, eds., *Mondrian/Nicholson: In Parallel* (London: Courtauld Gallery, 2012).

was as a sort of comradely greeting to Gabo, who had moved to London the year before.[27] Gabo was a leading representative of what was starting to be recognized internationally as constructivism. The subtitle of *Circle—International Survey of Constructive Art*—should thus be read as a statement of solidarity.

Although *Circle* seems benignly inclusive in tone and appearance, this was part of its covert polemic. Besides being internationally famous, Gabo was intensely controversial—and *Circle* staked a position in this controversy. Gabo brought with him to London an atmosphere of both revolutionary potential and artistic betrayal of the highest order. He had previously taught alongside other notorious avant-garde figures like Vladimir Tatlin, Wassily Kandinsky, and Alexander Rodchenko at Vkhutemas, the famed Higher Art and Technical Studios in Moscow, an institution set up in the aftermath of the revolution of 1917. From the vantage point of Britain, post-revolutionary Russia appeared to be embroiled in an ongoing debate about the relationship between forms of artistic production and forms of social organization.[28] (This was played out spectacularly in the Palace of the Soviets competition, for example in the gulf between Le Corbusier's 1931 scheme, a skeletal construction, and the socialist realist tower that won out.) The mythos of constructivism matched the stakes involved: A number of artists and architects in Russia had met their tragic demise after finding themselves in untenable ideological positions when the political winds changed.[29] When he moved to London some twenty years later, Gabo arrived into a situation in which such artistic-political experimentation seemed to fall outside the realm of possibility. Summerson would later lampoon the

---

27 Martin, "Introduction."

28 See Benjamin H.D. Buchloh, "Cold War Constructivism," in *Reconstructing Modernism: Art in New York, Paris, and Montreal, 1945–1964*, ed. Serge Guilbaut (Cambridge, MA: MIT Press, 1990), 85–112.

29 See Yve-Alain Bois, "Russian Revolution: On the Politics of Constructivism," *Artforum* 44, no. 6 (February 2006): 53–58.

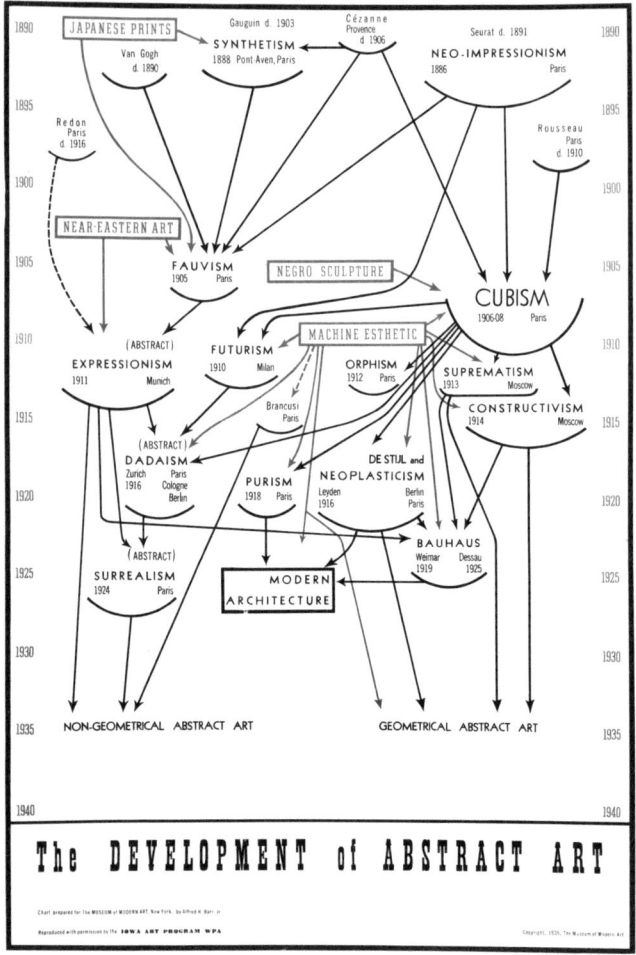

2 Alfred H. Barr, Jr., *The Development of Abstract Art*, 1936

halfhearted "ideologies" of British modernist architects in this period, and the casual sense of "brotherhood" and "discipline" to which they held.[30] In short, Gabo's westward move appeared to come along with an embrace of casualness, a shedding of politics, and a turn to "art for art's sake" that would appear to former colleagues and contemporary critics as inexcusable apostasy.[31]

Although *Circle* should be understood as a further gambit in the string of battles and betrayals that animated constructivism, its connotations were very different in the world of architecture than in the world of art. The central contradiction of Gabo's life and work—flip-flopping between "construction" and "composition"—serves as a case in point:

> For the Constructivists, the traditional order of composition was what had to be destroyed—because both the subjective arbitrariness of the aesthetic choices it elicited, and the age-old conventions of its formal devices (balance, hierarchy), were for them ciphers of the authoritarian social order of the Czarist regime and had no place in a revolutionary society. They went to great lengths to find ways in which one could motivate the organization of a work of art according to the properties of its material and the process in use: it is the motivated, "objective" organization (as opposed to the subjective, arbitrary composition) that they called a construction.[32]

Construction was thus a practice meant to undermine the traditional art object. The widespread "return to order" in art—of which Gabo was a prime representative in the 1930s—was also a return to composition and a rejection of the objective and the political in favor of subjective, apolitical

30 Summerson, "Introduction," 14–15.
31 See Hill, "Constructivism"; Buchloh, "Cold War Constructivism."
32 Hal Foster et al., *Art since 1900: Modernism, Antimodernism, Postmodernism* (London: Thames & Hudson, 2004), 290.

contemplation. *Circle*'s rhetoric of unity appears, in this light, as a stark renunciation of divisive political convictions. It also appears strikingly blind to the chaos that characterized Europe in the 1930s: If there was ever a time to be politically engaged, it was 1937.[33]

The opposition between composition and construction (or, in other words: art as disinterested contemplation versus art as political action) crops up repeatedly in the pages of *Circle*, but the architectural work in the volume did not fit neatly within these artistic pigeonholes. Compare, for instance, the essays in *Circle* by Mondrian and Le Corbusier.[34] Mondrian's essay, "Plastic Art and Pure Plastic Art," reads as a definitive statement of an uncompromising artistic project.[35] Parts of it come across as inscrutable koans—"Non-figurative art is created by establishing *a dynamic rhythm of determinate mutual relations* which *excludes the formation of any particular form*"—but its conclusion could hardly be more clear: "What is certain is that no escape is possible for the non-figurative artist: he *must stay within his field and march towards the consequences of his art.*"[36] Mondrian fostered millennial ambitions: "In a future perhaps remote, ... a new plastic reality will be created" in which architecture, sculpture, and painting will be unified into a "*purely constructive*" practice.[37]

---

33 Or so the argument goes. This is implicit in Buchloh's argument in "Cold War Constructivism" and the ethos of the October group of art critics—even the name "October" sides with the revolution. Rosalind Krauss, "About October," *October* 1 (1976): 3. A counterargument might insist that, in the context of England on the precipice of war, advocating for order was a political choice equivalent to siding with parliamentary democracy against communist and fascist radicalism—not necessarily a bad choice. For artists and architects, it meant fighting for a relatively autonomous space in which to do work that might otherwise be coopted by patriotism and propaganda.

34 Piet Mondrian, "Plastic Art and Pure Plastic Art (Figurative Art and Non-Figurative Art)," in *Circle: International Survey of Constructive Art*, ed. Leslie Martin, Ben Nicholson, and Naum Gabo (London: Faber & Faber, 1937), 41–56; and Le Corbusier, "The Quarrel with Realism: The Destiny of Painting," in *Circle: International Survey of Constructive Art*, ed. Leslie Martin, Ben Nicholson, and Naum Gabo (London: Faber & Faber, 1937), 67–74.

35 Foster et al., *Art since 1900*, 286–89.

36 Mondrian, "Plastic Art," 49, 56.

37 Mondrian, "Plastic Art," 56.

(Incidentally, this is one meaning of the term "program" in the context of art. An artistic program is a project, a set of principles, and a battle waged by the artist toward a more-or-less utopian goal. Mondrian's Neoplasticism epitomized programmatic artistic practice. Art theorists continue to look back with the tug of nostalgia to a time when artists believed in revolutionary causes and acted on those beliefs. This notion of program is now referred to in architecture as "having a project."[38])

Le Corbusier's essay in *Circle* falls on the opposite end of the spectrum, far from "construction" and in the realm of "composition" and compromise. It reads as a plea not to spoil the architect's pristine walls: "I love walls beautifully proportioned and dread to see them given over to minds unprepared."[39] Le Corbusier does not imagine a difficult march toward the artwork of the future, but instead opines that cubism has already "opened the gates to the universality of the great periods of art" by expressing "the strength of geometry [and] symbolism."[40] As commentators have stressed, a more generic and compromised statement of cubism would be difficult to imagine.[41]

While *Circle* is permeated with lingering tensions between strong programs and pragmatic compromises, it is notable that the British artists and architects included in the volume fall reliably on the side of the reasonable. The editor of the *Architectural Review*, J. M. Richards, contributed an essay on "The Condition of Architecture and the Principle of Anonymity" that takes such an aerial view of the battlefield of

38 See Antoine Picon, "The Ghost of Architecture: The Project and Its Codification," *Perspecta* 35 (2004): 8–19.

39 Le Corbusier, "Quarrel with Realism," 72.

40 Le Corbusier, "Quarrel with Realism," 73.

41 One important survey mocks the "vagueness" of Le Corbusier's "middlebrow, academicized version of geometric abstraction that has no programmatic characteristic other than that of being 'non-objective,' to use the vocabulary of the period." Foster et al., *Art since 1900*, 287. We might reply, however, that both pure compositions and pure constructions are out of the question in architecture: architecture is in the business of satisfying clients, not affirming or destroying figurative art.

avant-garde practice that evidence of conflict is scarcely legible.[42] Nicholson, the consummate British artist, contributed four short quotations that add up to the most basic description of aesthetic experience conceivable.[43] Amid this morass of compromise, Martin's essay is perhaps the most striking. He takes cues from industrial designers and engineers, who have already, he says, "exploded the belief in appearance" within their disciplines.[44] To this commonplace observation (which echoes Le Corbusier in *Vers une architecture*), Martin contributes the idea that architects should serve only as "coordinators." This notion adds a second layer of anonymity on top of the anonymous appearance of engineered objects. The expertise of the architect, according to Martin, lies not in designing beautiful buildings, but in planning humane environments:

> The modern building is essentially a part of the town planned as a healthy working unity, not merely another building in a vast spread of the unplanned in which the occasional vista and the imposing revivalist facade make a last despairing effort to "keep up appearances."[45]

While Le Corbusier argued for an "engineer's aesthetic," Martin proposes that architects ignore aesthetics altogether and turn instead to the practices of engineering and planning.

The other texts in *Circle* confirm the impression that modern architecture was systematically in favor of

---

42 J.M. Richards, "The Condition of Architecture and the Principle of Anonymity," in *Circle: International Survey of Constructive Art*, ed. Leslie Martin, Ben Nicholson, and Naum Gabo (London: Faber & Faber, 1937), 184–89.

43 Ben Nicholson, "Quotations," in *Circle: International Survey of Constructive Art*, ed. Leslie Martin, Ben Nicholson, and Naum Gabo (London: Faber & Faber, 1937), 75.

44 Leslie Martin, "The State of Transition," in *Circle: International Survey of Constructive Art*, ed. Leslie Martin, Ben Nicholson, and Naum Gabo (London: Faber & Faber, 1937), 215–19, here 215.

45 Martin, "State of Transition," 218.

anonymity. Writing about the influential Congrès Internationaux d'Architecture Moderne, Sigfried Giedion flatly states that "C.I.A.M. tries as far as possible to eliminate personal work."[46] Walter Gropius, in an essay on architectural education, insists that "no longer must the isolated individual work continue to occupy pride of place, but rather the creation of the generally valid type, the development towards a standard."[47] Lewis Mumford concurs:

> The human impulse to create everlasting monuments springs perhaps out of the desire for the living to perpetuate themselves .... The very notion of a modern monument is a contradiction in terms: if it is a monument, it cannot be modern, and if it is modern, it cannot be a monument.[48]

Taken together, these essays add up to a polemic about the values and the essence of modern architecture. As Summerson would later remind his readers, given a choice between individual expression and anonymous coordination, modernists would (or should) always side with the latter.[49]

This central tension of 1930s modernism—composition vs. construction, expression vs. coordination—established the atmosphere into which *Data* arrived thirty years later. Like *Circle*, *Data* was initiated and edited by an artist, and it brought together projects and statements from about two dozen contributors across creative fields. Also like *Circle*, *Data* was largely ignored when it was published, and it

---

46 Si[e]gfried Giedion, "The Work of the C.I.A.M," in *Circle: International Survey of Constructive Art*, ed. Leslie Martin, Ben Nicholson, and Naum Gabo (London: Faber & Faber, 1937), 272–78, here 274.

47 Walter Gropius, "Art Education and State," in *Circle: International Survey of Constructive Art*, ed. Leslie Martin, Ben Nicholson, and Naum Gabo (London: Faber & Faber, 1937), 238–42, here 239.

48 Lewis Mumford, "The Death of the Monument," in *Circle: International Survey of Constructive Art*, ed. Leslie Martin, Ben Nicholson, and Naum Gabo (London: Faber & Faber, 1937), 263–70, here 263.

49 Summerson, "Introduction."

appears now as a time capsule of a peculiar—and relatively unknown—artistic subculture.[50]

The most immediately apparent novelty of *Data* is its aura of computation. It is little more than an aura, however: no computers were actually involved. The term "data" refers, of course, to the raw material of the information age—the very stuff of computation—and *Data* leans on this connotation.[51] Its title is even styled in capital letters—DATA—that look like the logos of IBM and DEC, the major computer manufacturers of the era. By the 1960s, an orderly sans-serif aesthetic had become the commonplace graphic identifier of techno-modernity through the effort of marketing firms and designers trained at schools founded in the wake of the Bauhaus—the Hochschule für Gestaltung in Ulm and the New Bauhaus in Chicago, for instance.[52] (Although the graphic designer of *Data*, Richard Hollis, was initially trained in a traditional idiom, he picked up the new Swiss typography from the local concrete poetry scene and a visit to constructivists in Paris.[53]) Despite these trappings, the text of *Data* rarely mentions computation, and the title serves only as a ritual invocation of contemporary culture. The volume appeared at a moment of peak optimism in the computer industry, before the software crisis of the early 1970s and a sharp turn to techno-pessimism.[54] It is worth recalling the mood:

---

50 Unlike *Circle*, *Data* has not really been rediscovered after more than fifty years. See more on the volume in Hill, "Editor's Forward."

51 On the evolution of the term, see Daniel Rosenberg, "Data before the Fact," in *Raw Data Is an Oxymoron*, ed. Lisa Gitelman (Cambridge, MA: MIT Press, 2013), 15–40.

52 See, e.g., the work of Eliot Noyes for IBM; Noyes was trained as an architect at the Harvard Graduate School of Design by Walter Gropius and Marcel Breuer, both former Bauhausler. See John Harwood, *The Interface: IBM and the Transformation of Corporate Design, 1945–1976* (Minneapolis: University of Minnesota Press, 2016).

53 See Christopher Wilson, "Reputations: Richard Hollis," *Eye* 15, no. 59 (2006): 26–35. See more on concrete poetry in the chapter "Structuralist Activity in *Form*" in the book at hand.

54 Martin Campbell-Kelly, *From Airline Reservations to Sonic the Hedgehog: A History of the Software Industry* (Cambridge, MA: MIT Press, 2003).

> A dream of technical control and of instant information conveyed at unthought-of velocities haunted Sixties culture. The wired, electronic outlines of a cybernetic society became apparent .... It was a technologically utopian structure of feeling, positivistic and "scientistic".[55]

Techno-scientific optimism in the 1960s British art world was tempered by the shadow of the modernist avant-garde, represented by *Circle*. When the art scene reconvened after the wartime lull, the first generation of abstractionists—figures like Nicholson and Gabo—were in the position of consolidating their legacy. Younger artists were acutely aware of their status as newcomers to a venerable tradition, and they sought to reinvigorate the movement on the global stage.[56] Mondrian had died in 1944, Gabo had moved to Connecticut in 1946, and Nicholson had relocated to St Ives in 1939, turning to more naturalistic themes in his painting and becoming an ever more parochial figure. The orthodoxies of modernism were increasingly felt as stifling constraints, and it became ever clearer what would be required to re-establish constructivism as a viable program.

The first step was to historicize interwar modernism—to identify and summarize its main tenets before moving beyond them. The editor of *Data*, Anthony Hill, was at the forefront of this effort. Hill finished his studies in 1951 at a Bauhaus-inspired course at the Central School of Art in London taught by Victor Pasmore, who was developing an abstract style of painting stimulated by the *Circle* group. Hill became the youngest of a new group of artists under Pasmore's influence. He took to traveling regularly to Paris to meet with the likes of Francis Picabia, František Kupka, and Georges Vantongerloo, and he initiated correspondences with Marcel

---

55 David Mellor, *The Sixties Art Scene in London* (London: Phaidon, 1993), 107.

56 See Alastaire Grieve, *Constructed Abstract Art in England After the Second World War: A Neglected Avant-Garde* (New Haven: Yale University Press, 2005).

Duchamp, Max Bill, and Charles Biederman.[57] This put Hill in an ideal position to observe both "what constructivism *was*" and "what it *is*." Two years before editing *Data*, he wrote in *Studio International* that

> by 1923 or so constructivism applied to plastic art is identified with the activity of artists who were mainly concerned in laying the foundation of *a new plastic art*. These activities tended to merge with those of other artists, principally the neo-plasticists (the De Stijl and its aftermath) having the same concerns—that is, being preoccupied with an all embracing philosophy of modern art. After the war, against the background of an intense interest and feeling of solidarity towards much of the ethos of pre-war constructivism, artists were again taking up basically the same programmes.[58]

While postwar constructivism was animated by the same "philosophy of art" as the pre-war movement, Hill observed that the lineage had split in two directions in recent decades. He summarized what had happened in reference to Gabo and his former compatriot, El Lissitzky: "Very broadly Lissitzky apart from his notably original life's work, represents a type of constructivism that appears to have melted away (the collectivist, ideological and internationally oriented), while Gabo represents one part of the other side."[59] Through this bit of slapdash historiography, Hill found an opening for contemporary artists: taking up the "other part" of the non-political project of constructivism, adjacent to Gabo but somehow different.

Data illuminates the path that Hill considered the most productive way to continue modernist experimentation into the 1960s. The volume collects the work of the Construc-

---

57 Grieve, *Constructed Abstract Art in England*, 107.
58 Hill, "Constructivism," 142.
59 Hill, "Constructivism," 141.

tionist Group, the clique gathered around Pasmore. Even the term itself—constructionism—was an attempt by the artists to distance themselves from the popular (and in their view mistaken) understanding of constructivism as a vaguely "all-embracing philosophy of modern art," as Hill put it, and to return to the original principles of "construction" as they had been hashed out in revolutionary Russia. Along with Hill, about half of the contributors to *Data* were avowed Constructionists. Most of the others were older Europeans—members of what would soon be called "the historical avant-garde"—although a few outliers made their way in as well, notably the two main contributors of architectural work, Constant Nieuwenhuys and Yona Friedman (about whom more in a moment).[60]

Hill described the output of constructionism in broad though exacting terms: *Data* presents "an attitude of mind expressed through a variety of physical propositions."[61] Unlike *Circle*, *Data* eschews traditional categorization and presents artists with little discernible order, and it is often unclear whether the artworks are sculptural objects, models of buildings, or something else entirely. But the attitudes and allegiances of *Data* are clear enough, combing the visual material of De Stijl (rectangular blocks of primary colors) with the handmade sensibility of, say, Vladimir Tatlin's multimaterial constructions.

The Constructionists inherited from interwar modernism the sense that their multi-media experimentation would culminate in architecture—but only after expectations as to what constitutes "architecture" had been recast. This cherished dream of modernism was aptly represented by the diagram of the Bauhaus curriculum that places "building" as the shared core concern of the school's various material investigations, and it was the aim of its messianic ethos: "Together let us desire, conceive, and create the new

60 See Peter Bürger, *Theorie der Avantgarde* (Frankfurt: Suhrkamp, 1974).
61 Hill, "Constructivism," 142.

structure of the future, which will embrace architecture and sculpture and painting in one unity and which will one day rise toward heaven from the hands of a million workers like the crystal symbol of a new faith."[62] Writing in this vein in his programmatic statement in *Circle*, Mondrian had likewise called for the "unification of architecture, sculpture and painting" into "a new plastic reality"; artistic production would result not in an artwork but in "the creation of an atmosphere."[63] In Britain circa 1960, Mondrian's manifesto was echoed in Summerson's vision of associating architects not with the traditionally limited realm of architecture—for "clients in the aristocracy, the City and the Church"—but with "the whole material environment" and "every building activity in the country."[64]

These ambitions render less anomalous the work of *Data*'s two "experimental urbanists," Constant and Friedman. Constant first met Hill and other Constructionists during a trip to London in 1956, shortly after he had abandoned painting in favor of three-dimensional work and the same year he began his New Babylon project, a "future society ... in which labour and creation will be synonymous" depicted in a series of models, drawings, and collages.[65] Photos of several of these models made their way into the pages of *Data*.[66] With wires strung between looping frameworks, some recall Gabo's constructions (fig. 3). Others add platforms and scale-model automobiles to situate them firmly in the world of inhabitable buildings. A model of a concert hall for electronic music features rounded plexiglass and thin

[62] Walter Gropius, "Programme of the Staatliches Bauhaus in Weimar," in *Programs and Manifestoes on 20th-Century Architecture*, ed. Ulrich Conrads (Cambridge, MA: MIT Press, 1971), 49–53, here 49.

[63] Mondrian, "Plastic Art," 56.

[64] Summerson, "Introduction," 27; Summerson, "Bread & Butter," 237.

[65] Mark Wigley, "Paper, Scissors, Blur," in *The Activist Drawing: Retracing Situationist Architectures from Constant's New Babylon to Beyond* (Cambridge, MA: MIT Press, 1998), 27–56, here 27.

[66] Constant Nieuwenhuys, "About the Meaning of Construction," in *Data: Directions in Art, Theory and Aesthetics*, ed. Anthony Hill (London: Faber & Faber, 1968), 175–79, here 176.

steel supports that suggest the pneumatic structures and tension cables of Ivan Leonidov's Lenin Institute proposal of 1927. Destruction and reconstruction are also thematized: In one model, crumbly plaster buildings are scattered on an otherwise empty ground plane, with a shiny steel and plexiglass construction hovering above. The proposal employs the same visual-rhetorical trick used by Ludwig Mies van der Rohe in his Friedrichstrasse Skyscraper model of 1922, transposed in Constant's case into a seemingly post-apocalyptic zone. Another model projects a grid over the ground plane, charting an abstract territory for the superimposition of ephemeral constructions by nomadic inhabitants.

In the text accompanying his projects, Constant reiterates a fundamental principle of constructivism: that the goal is not to create objects of aesthetic contemplation but to unite creative production with social life. Like Hill, Constant is skeptical of the old political project of constructivism:

> The meaning of constructivism in our day is essentially other than that of the constructivist movement in the beginning of this century. The process of mechanisation in the higher developed countries has gone so far now that human labour will no longer be the principal force of production. Automation, especially, allows an increase of free time that makes the idealisation of labour senseless. The main problem of our time is not the organisation of the industrial work but the recreation of the unemployed "worker." But a worker who is unemployed continuously ceases to be a worker. Not the labourer but the player, not "homo faber" but "homo ludens" is the type of man to whom the future belongs.[67]

Constant's models evoke the post-industrial, post-work world of *homo ludens*. He employs the hand-built aesthetic of earlier constructivism but shifts its connotation from

---

67 Nieuwenhuys, "About the Meaning of Construction," 176.

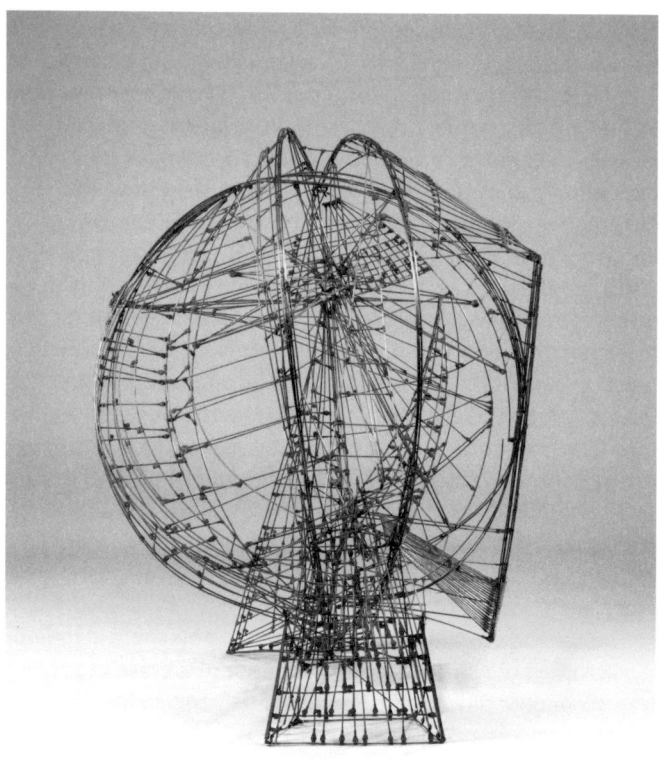

3 Constant [Nieuwenhuys], *Ruimtecircus II*, 1958-1959

work to play. (This also resolved a lingering contradiction of the machine aesthetic, in which finely hand-built objects incongruously emulated the often-brutal products of manufacturing.) In *Data*, Constant presents not an empty universal space fit for factory or office work but an intricate jungle gym suitable for individualized self-fulfillment.

The criticism launched at Constant within his own milieu of continental Europe suggests a problem that would confront the Constructionists and other artists riding the 1960s wave of techno-optimism. The rhetorical shift from working to playing renders all the more obvious the disconnect between constructivist ambitions and mundane realities. Communism had not arrived; everyone was not engaged in perpetual play. If a project is not about the artwork itself but the revolution in which it plays is a part, as Constant and the earlier constructivists insisted, did this not mean that art is strictly impossible if the revolution is not underway? This was the essence of Guy Debord's criticism of Constant:

> Constant's work, in its unfinished, "scale model" aspect … perfectly illustrates the falsity of bourgeois artistic freedom. The artist has, at best, the freedom to ply his trade as an artist, that is, to carry out normalized production, matching the needs of a given stratum of the dominant culture's highly differentiated public. A truly vanguard project today poses the problem of the new trades, which can hardly be exercised within the frame of bourgeois society.[68]

The difference of opinion between Constant and Debord—which was a divisive affair at the time—stood as an important lesson for the Constructionist Group, the lesson being that it is difficult to know the motives driving an artistic process from its results.[69]

68 Guy Debord, "Constant and the Path of Unitary Urbanism," trans. Brian Holms, *NOT BORED!* 28 (1997), http://www.notbored.org/constant-debord.html.
69 See Catherine de Zegher and Mark Wigley, eds., *The Activist Drawing:*

In this regard, it is worth comparing Constant with *Data*'s other "experimental urbanist," Yona Friedman. Friedman was a Hungarian architect who moved to Paris in 1957; his Spatial City project embodies the principles of what he called "mobile architecture." Friedman's work is in some ways uncannily similar to Constant's: Both envisioned airy, ramshackle constructions suspended above a gritty former world, and both suggested that their new constructions were calibrated to a utopic society yet to come. Friedman's drawings were, however, the only diagrammatic sketches published in *Data*—and in their genre they appear exactly opposite to Constant's highly concrete constructions. (Concrete and constructed, that is, as the opposite of abstract.) Friedman cheerfully outlines megastructures crisscrossing the globe and drawing people together in Venn diagrams of shared humanity. Problems that to others appear intractable (until the revolution, at least) are rhetorically "solved" through design applied at the scale of the globe.

With ironic succinctness, Hill summarizes the generic "social ethic" deployed by Friedman as "a revolutionary art for a revolutionary concept of society"—as if the political and material messiness of the world could be simply reconceptualized and designed away in one fell swoop.[70] If this is the "all-embracing philosophy of modern art," how can we judge whether an artistic practice really is revolutionary?

The projects of Constant and Friedman highlight the contradictions the Constructionists faced when working at the scale of the problem itself—the scale of society—but "the social" need not be approached through design of the social totality; it can also be approached through individual microsocial encounters. Work commensurate with the human perceptual environment was more typical in *Data*. The first project in the volume, by Georges Vantongerloo, is a case

---

Retracing Situationist Architectures from Constant's New Babylon to Beyond (Cambridge, MA: MIT Press, 2001), 100–102.

70 Hill, "Constructivism," 142.

in point. Vantongerloo was an elder statesman of modern art who rose to fame in the 1910s while collaborating with Mondrian, Theo van Doesburg, and Bart van der Leck on the seminal magazine *De Stijl*. In *Data*, Vantongerloo contributed photographs of several "objects in plastic material," including *No. 214 (Cocon, Chrysalide, Embroyonnaire)*, a glass rod twisted in upon itself to form a loose spherical knot then suspended in the air by an invisible wire. The artwork is not the thing itself, however, but the experience of light as it passes through the floating, rotating object. With the help of his photographer, Vantongerloo attempts to capture the experience in a darkened room with careful lighting and a long exposure time, registering a circular blur of light (fig. 4). This is kinetic art, a temporal phenomenon.

Many Constructionists created art in this way, by setting up a device of some sort to create a finely calibrated and fleeting perceptual effect. Hill saw this as a fundamental aspect of "the constructivist syndrome," as he called it, and he pointed to László Moholy-Nagy's *Light Space Modulator* as a key example (fig. 5). Hill cites Moholy-Nagy's address to the Bauhaus on "the spiritual and social aspects of constructivist art": "Constructive art is processual, forever open in all directions. It is a builder of man's ability to perceive, to react emotionally and to reason logically."[71] If the traditional art object is beyond redemption, the mechanics of perceptual experience could take its place as the object of artistic ambition.

This attitude, which was shared by the Constructionists, had far-reaching consequences for developments in aesthetics after the Second World War. The messianic drive of Mondrian's struggle to obliterate composition faded even as his call for "a new plastic reality" became

---

71 Hill, "Constructivism," 142–44. Moholy-Nagy was a pivotal figure between prewar German aesthetics and the more wide-reaching (and ultimately ubiquitous) aesthetics of "technology" in the postwar period. Alena Williams, "Movement in Vision: Cinema, Aesthetics, and Modern German Culture, 1918–1933," PhD thesis (Columbia University, 2014).

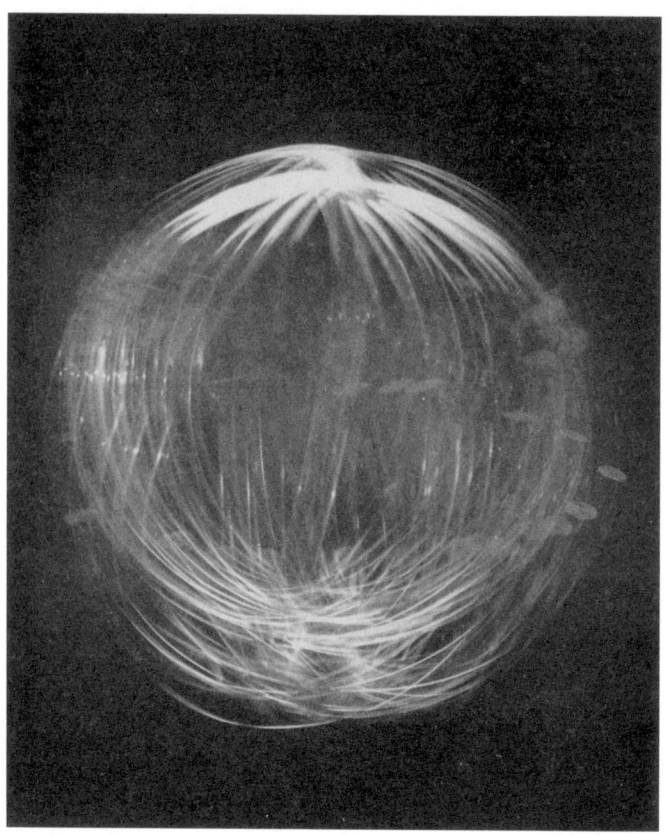

4   Georges Vantongerloo, *No. 214 (Cocon, Chrysalide, Embroyonnaire)*, 1950

FROM *CIRCLE* TO *DATA*: AVANT-GARDE ROUTINES

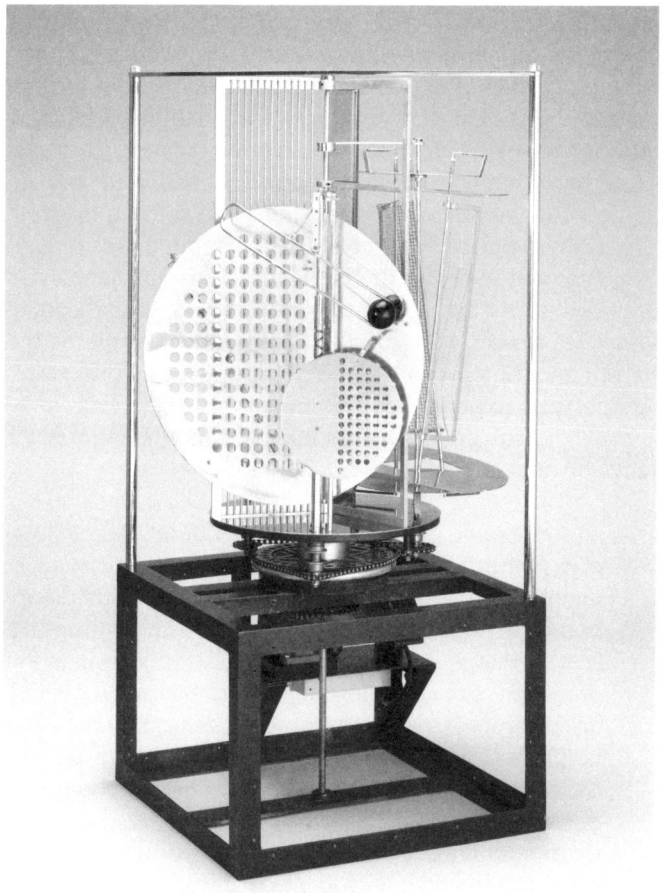

5 László Moholy-Nagy, *Light Space Modulator*, 1930

an increasingly common ambition. In an artwork that is completely ephemeral—merely a temporary effect of light——the platitudes of compositional art are utterly out of the question. Once this shift had been affected, however, a new question arises: Visual phenomena are something to marvel at, certainly, but how are they to be evaluated? And how are perceptual effects to be judged alongside social effects?

For a sketch of this problem in architecture, we can turn for a moment to one of the most iconic essays of the era's architectural theory, Colin Rowe's "Mathematics of the Ideal Villa." The essay is remarkable for the way it conflates the formal and the functional by placing both in an uneasy relationship to experience. This begins with a binary Rowe introduces in an epigraph from the eighteenth-century architect Christopher Wren:

> There are two causes of beauty—natural and customary. Natural [beauty] is from geometry consisting in uniformity, that is equality and proportion. Customary beauty is begotten by the use, as familiarity breeds a love to things not in themselves lovely. Here lies the great occasion of errors, but always the true test is natural or geometrical beauty. Geometrical figures are naturally more beautiful than irregular ones: the square, the circle are the most beautiful, next the parallelogram and the oval. There are only two beautiful positions of straight lines, perpendicular and horizontal; this is from Nature and consequently necessity, no other than upright being firm.[72]

Building on Wren's distinction, the bulk of Rowe's essay is an extended exercise in compare-and-contrast between villas by Le Corbusier and Palladio on the full range of connota-

---

72 Christopher Wren, *Parentalia* (London: Osborn, 1750), 351. Quoted in Colin Rowe, "The Mathematics of the Ideal Villa: Palladio and Le Corbusier Compared," *Architectural Review* 101 (March 1947): 101–4, here 101.

tions of "natural beauty" and "conventional beauty." The first of these terms was bound to call for interpretive gymnastics because the idea of natural beauty combines, in its two words, both function and form: the functional necessity of "natural" laws and subjective character of the experience of "beautiful" form.[73] The concept of natural beauty is related, of course, to the "mathematics" in the title of Rowe's essay, and more specifically to geometry—and even more precisely to proportion. Following Wren, Rowe suggests that beauty can be found in the natural world because the universe is pervaded by proportional regularity. This is an old idea, as old as geometry itself. What is important to note here is that this idea runs counter to the more typical conceptual division of modernism (which was introduced in Summerson's terms in the Prologue). For Summerson, the visual aspect of architecture—its "play of volumes ... beneath the light"—is governed by convention; Summerson thus interprets Le Corbusier as the inheritor of the conventions of rationalism and "the classical language of architecture," with which he works as a "poet innovator."[74] *Visual*, *formal*, *conventional*, and *beautiful* go together in this formulation. The natural world is something else entirely for Summerson, and he argues that a completely different evaluative framework is required for working with functional programs. *Biological*, *functional*, *objective*, and *programmatic* are on the other side of Summerson's conceptual dichotomy. (This is his version of form versus function.)

To claim that the natural world has its own type of beauty, as Rowe does, is to claim that, in Summerson's terms, the "missing language" of modernism has been found, and

---

[73] This is also the contradiction at the heart of Immanuel Kant's aesthetic theory, which is based on "subjectively universal" judgements—that is, personal and unverifiable judgements that are nevertheless thought to be universally valid. See, e.g., Robert Hanna, "Kant's Theory of Judgment," in *Stanford Encyclopedia of Philosophy*, 2017, https://plato.stanford.edu/archives/win2017/entries/kant-judgment/.

[74] Summerson, *Classical Language*; Summerson, "Bread & Butter," 233.

that it is a language of geometry and proportion. This is what is implied by the concept of natural beauty. Rowe suggests, moreover, that this language is not ruled by customary conventions (as human languages usually are), but rather that it is universal. Extrapolating from Rowe then, we begin to imagine a lineage of architecture running from Palladio to Le Corbusier that developed a way of working with the universal language of mathematics to create a realm of objective beauty.

The concept of natural beauty as it relates to geometrical proportions was a subject of much debate in the years after Rowe's essay.[75] Its consequences were various. A facade can be both experienced and visually decoded; if it is governed by natural beauty, it will be there for all to see. Proportionality, in this case, is a direct visual experience. This was how Le Corbusier worked with proportion in his facades ruled by "regulating lines" (fig. 6). But can an architectural plan be beautiful in a similar sense? An architect looking at the plan might notice pleasing proportions, but is someone within a room of a villa supposed to somehow experience its proportionality? And does this manifest as an unconscious feeling of harmony or is it decoded more directly in conscious experience? Or, finally, if the proportionality of a room is not something that can be perceived, what bearing would it have on the "beauty" of the building at all? These slippages between the two aspects of Rowe's concept of natural beauty—the abstract / universal language of mathematics and the concrete / subjective realm of experience—signaled a deep (and productive) irresolution at the heart of his aesthetic theory.

With the Constructionist Group, this conceptual ambiguity became the locus of an artistic research program. How can an artist experiment with natural beauty? While the

---

75 One insightful debate took place in 1957: Nikolaus Pevsner, "Report of a Debate on the Motion 'That Systems of Proportion Make Good Design Easier and Bad Design More Difficult'," *Journal of the Royal Institute of British Architects* 64, no. 11 (September 1957): 456–63.

FROM *CIRCLE* TO *DATA*: AVANT-GARDE ROUTINES 41

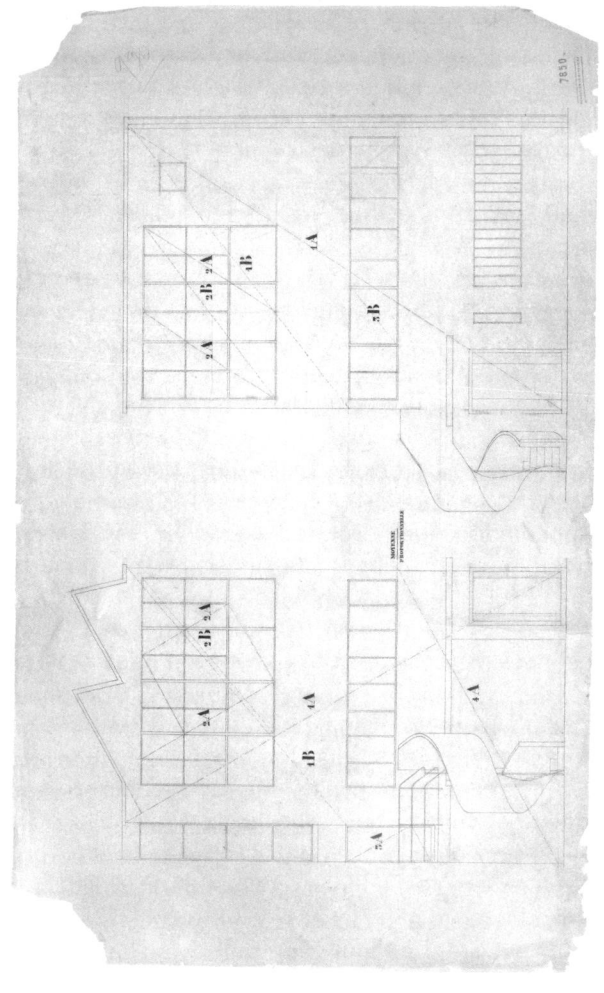

6 Le Corbusier, "Regulating lines," 1923

editors of *Circle* blandly sought to unify "the field of art" with "the branches of science," Hill's editorial statement for *Data* refers to an intricate "cross-section of related movements" to be explored: On the side of art are "constructive, concrete, kinetic, structuralist and synthesist" varieties, to which he adds "specialists" from "interrelated fields of interest to plasticians," namely "philosophy, mathematics, physics, engineering, sociology, and urbanism."[76]

The closest *Data* comes to offering a manifesto on how artistic "specialists" should approach this expanded field of natural beauty is in the volume's opening essay by the Dutch mathematician and philosopher Bertus Brouwer. Brouwer admonishes readers not to talk about "science" but instead to focus on "scientific thinking," which is "an economical and efficient way [of cataloguing] extensive groups of co-operative causal sequences" and is "based on mathematics."[77] Brouwer reminds us that mathematics is not monolithic, but rather a burgeoning field made up of numerous "mathematical species." This suggests a direction for artists: If scientists investigate and explain causal sequences, artists can likewise tinker with them, making art using mathematics to control chains of cause and effect. The highest beauty, Brouwer says, is "the introspectional beauty of mathematics," when "the basic intuition of mathematics is left to free unfolding."[78] The mathematically minded artist is thus someone who reveals the mechanics of the natural-mathematical world by "unfolding" it within an artwork.

New techniques can aid in this mathematical / artistic investigation. Vantongerloo describes how instruments allow both scientists and artists to narrow their focus from bland universals to intriguing particulars. He begins by noting dryly that "man has five senses, and they suit him

---

76 Martin, Nicholson, and Gabo, *Circle*, v; Hill, "Editor's Forward," here 5.

77 L. E. J. Brouwer, "Consciousness, Philosophy and Mathematics," in *Data: Directions in Art, Theory and Aesthetics*, ed. Anthony Hill (London: Faber & Faber, 1968), 12–21, here 14.

78 Brouwer, "Consciousness, Philosophy and Mathematics," here 15–16.

well,"[79] but this dull universality quickly devolves as he begins to speculate on the marvels of the physical universe. Contemplating the beauty of spheres, Vantongerloo turns immediately to concrete examples: "The sun has its different atmospheres, its photosphere, chromosphere, its crown and its protuberances. Jupiter is only a gas."[80] The only hope we have of understanding the world around us is by using specialized instruments:

> Now one has much more contact with the universe through radio electricity, the radio telescope, radar. One must use the same language as creation in order to be able to synchronise with it .... Couldn't one send waves into the universe which would send back information to us on the characteristics of the stars?[81]

Close interrogation of the "language of creation" produces an opening for an unusual type of artwork: Artists can make instruments to probe perceptual possibilities and the limits of human understanding. This is how to understand Vantongerloo's rotating glass knots: as instruments of research into natural beauty.

Extrapolating from Brouwer and Vantongerloo, then, we can understand the Constructionist Group as starting at the "geometrical" branch of Barr's genealogy of modern art (see fig. 2) and developing it along finer-grained branches of mathematical sub-species. This is reflected in the artworks collected in *Data*, with their various mathematically inflected titles. The artist Richard Lohse prefers series and systems, as in his *Thirty systematic series of shades* and *16 progressive asymmetrical colour groups within a symmetrical system*. Mary Martin has groups, permutations, and rhythms.

---

79 Georges Vantongerloo, "To Perceive / Universal-Existence? / Conception of Space 1 / Conception of Space 2," in *Data: Directions in Art, Theory and Aesthetics*, ed. Anthony Hill (London: Faber & Faber, 1968), 22–40, here 22.

80 Vantongerloo, "To Perceive," 26.

81 Vantongerloo, "To Perceive," 26.

Francois Molnar has randomness and simulation. Kenneth Martin has oscillation; Francois Morellet, undulation. As these titles suggest, the Constructionists' mathematical references were diverse and far-reaching. Celebrated works by D'Arcy Thompson on morphology and Matila Ghyka on geometry were on their shelves, as were Theodore Cook's *Curves of Life* (1914), Jay Hambridge's *Elements of Dynamic Symmetry* (1926), John Power's *Les Éléments de la Construction Picturale* (1932), and many others (fig. 7).[82] Earlier modernists who had engaged with mathematics, however vaguely, also loomed large among their precedents. The work of Paul Klee had been featured in exhibitions in London beginning in the late 1940s and early 1950s—shows which the Constructionists eagerly attended (fig. 8).[83] Klee's *Pedagogical Sketchbook* was translated into English in 1953, and *The Thinking Eye*—in which he describes lines as the movement of points and drawing as "taking a line for a walk," among other geometrical aphorisms—was published in 1961.

Mathematics was the common denominator of Constructionist artistic practice, but the specifics of how it was used varied, and it was a matter of contentious debate. Some saw mathematics as little more than an inspiration. An oft-quoted statement by Ulm School of Design instructor Max Bill, to whom the Constructionists looked for guidance, captured this mood: "In my opinion it is possible to develop art on the basis of a mathematical way of thought ... . [It] is thought that makes it possible to organize emotional feelings into a work of art."[84] Kenneth Martin's stacks of blocks in a generally oscillating manner belong to this genre: They are loosely expressive of mathematical thoughts and feelings rather than embodying a strict numerical sequence or formula. Other Constructionists criticized this lackadaisical approach: "My argument against ... Gabo and Max Bill would be that they

---

82 Grieve, *Constructed Abstract Art in England*, 215.

83 Grieve, *Constructed Abstract Art in England*, 215–18.

84 Quoted in Anthony Hill, "Max Bill: The Search for the Unity of the Plastic Arts in Contemporary Life," *Typographica* 7 (1953): 21–28, here 23.

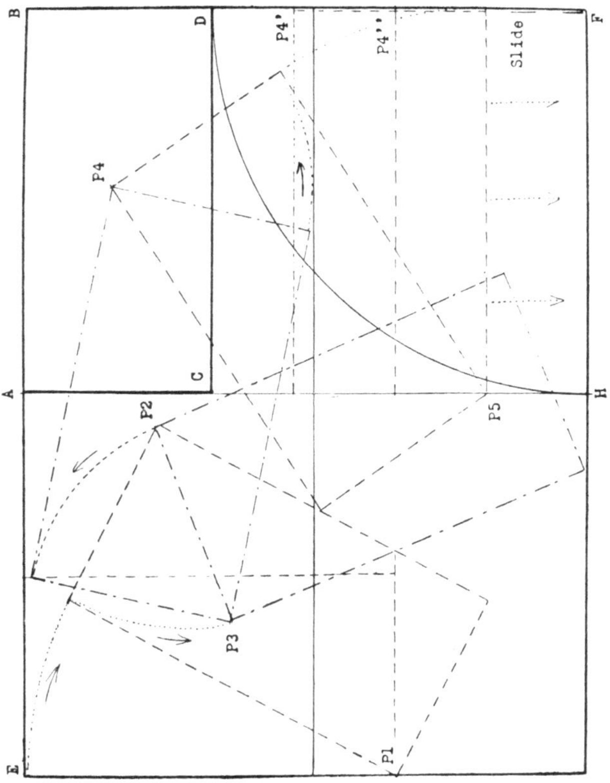

FROM *CIRCLE* TO *DATA*: AVANT-GARDE ROUTINES

7   J.W. Power, "The Moving Format," 1932

8 Paul Klee, *Botanical Garden, Section with the Ray-Leaved Plants*, 1946

were in love with the aesthetic beauty of mathematics rather than using mathematics as creative means."[85] Hill argued that artists should adhere to mathematical methods. Mary Martin concurred, describing her approach succinctly: "I start with a drawing, often suggested by a mathematical idea, which I carry forward to a precise concept of shape and form ... starting from one unit, subjecting it to a logic and accepting the result without any artistic interference."[86] Martin's *Expanding Form* illustrates the results of her method: A relief painting made of forms, governed by a mathematical series, appears as if generated by a complex sequences of unfolding and shifting operations (fig. 9). This artwork, which was typical of the Constructionist Group, was a direct response to Nicholson's earlier relief paintings—among the most celebrated works of British abstractionism—which have a handmade and subjective quality (fig. 10).

This borrowing of methods from mathematics sometimes led to a proceduralism of the studio. Photographs show Hill wearing a lab coat while carefully adjusting an artwork (fig. 11), and we imagine him sitting down as a mathematician to plan a series of exacting rules before switching to the persona of the lab technician to systematically carry them out. Constructionist projects often began with raw material from industrial manufacturing that would then be subject to a sequence of transformations based on an iconic mathematical formula or series (like the Fibonacci sequence).[87] The results, unsurprisingly, were almost invariably characterized by the precise repetition of elements, and works came in series of variations on themes. The projects in *Data* are consistently anti-figurative, like most of the work of

85 Anthony Hill, quoted in a 1954 letter to Charles Biederman. Grieve, *Constructed Abstract Art in England*, 225.

86 Quoted in Paul Overy, ed., *Mary Martin and Kenneth Martin: An Arts Council Touring Exhibition 1970–71* (London: Arts Council, 1970), 11. Also quoted in Alan Fowler, ed., *A Rational Aesthetic: The Systems Group and Associated Artists* (Southampton: Southampton City Art Gallery, 2008), 9.

87 Hill favored one-inch-by-one-inch L-shaped aluminum extrusions. Grieve, *Constructed Abstract Art in England*, 188.

9 Mary Martin, *Expanding Form*, 1954

FROM *CIRCLE* TO *DATA*: AVANT-GARDE ROUTINES

10 Ben Nicholson, *1934 (relief)*, 1934

Mondrian and Nicholson, but the Constructionists' bureaucratic impulse often rendered them anti-subjective in a way Nicholson, in particular, did not pursue. Constructionist artworks often appear routinized to the point of lifelessness—as if there were nothing artistic about them at all.

The contribution of the Constructionist Group—and its importance for the arrival of algorithmics into architecture—can be found in the group's investigation of mathematically regulated procedurality, which was an outcome of bureaucratic tendencies. A project by Vera and François Molnar midway through *Data* illustrates what proceduralism can uniquely accomplish. The accompanying text outlines the steps required to create a Mondrian-esque painting: Begin with a regular grid of identical graphical elements (short horizontal lines), and then rotate a randomly selected group of them by ninety degrees. The Molnars used this technique to create a provocatively dry approximation of Mondrian's *Composition No. 10 (Pier and Ocean)* of 1915. On the facing page, in a witty variation, some of the horizontal lines are swapped for diagonals (which would be heresy in Mondrian's Neoplasticism) (fig. 12). The Molnars thus proposed a critique—through the artwork itself—of Mondrian's mathematical mysticism.[88] While the spiritual dimension of abstractionism continued in Abstract Expressionism (for example with Mark Rothko), the Molnars liberated similar graphic material for more playful experimentation.

The Molnars' introduction of randomness into procedural composition served to remove the last major element of human choice from the process of painting, and their work can thus be seen as a culmination of the non-political project of constructivism that Hill had identified. (Choice still plays a role before the process begins, of course, when the artist chooses the rules and materials to be worked with.) In its context within *Data*, the Molnars' work is among the most

---

[88] On Mondrian's mysticism, see Hilton Kramer, "Mondrian & Mysticism: 'My Long Search Is Over,'" *New Criterion* 14 (September 1995): 4–14.

FROM *CIRCLE* TO *DATA*: AVANT-GARDE ROUTINES

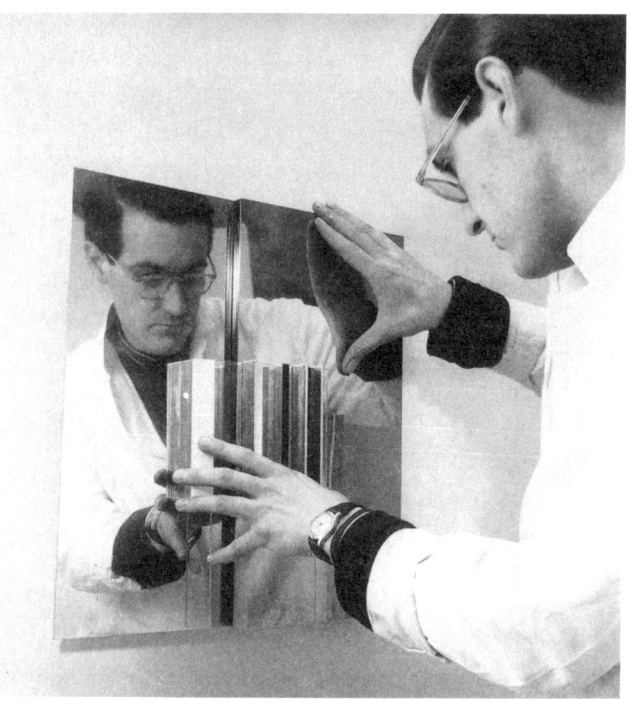

11 Anthony Hill adjusting his *Relief Construction*, c. 1957

12 Vera Molnar, *Untitled (Four elements distributed randomly)*, 1959

poignant: By thematizing freedom of choice through its absence, their work highlights a tension at the heart of the human condition. They suggest one approach to procedural aesthetics: Set up a rigorous field against which small variations register as moments of formal surprise and vitality. Not coincidentally, this is often described as the locus of beauty in mathematics. John Ernest phrased it in a way typical of his fellow Constructionists: "I suppose I am trying to achieve some of the beauty of a formal mathematical system in a visual experience, for it is this kind of beauty in mathematics—where the lovely abstract machinery goes into action—that moves me most deeply."[89]

Among the Constructionists, it was Hill who went furthest in the use of mathematical methods to engage with mathematical material in art. His essay in *Data* is a primer on graph theory that concludes in a remarkable study of topological symmetry and asymmetry in a painting by Mondrian. He begins by analyzing the topological network or graph that serves as the "infra-structure" of the painting, after which he produces a series of diagrams that represent the same network in five distinct ways—essentially sketching five Mondrian-esque paintings that would be both identical (in terms of topology) and distinct (in visual form) (fig. 13).[90] Hill ends with a striking speculation: He wonders whether the shared topographical features of the five possible Mondrians would be apparent in any way, even if only subconsciously.[91] (Here Hill echoes the questions implied by Rowe with respect to proportionality in architecture.) Would a new painting with the same topological structure be experienced as in some sense "the same" as Mondrian's painting? Does the topology

---

89 John Ernest, "Some Thoughts on Mathematics," *Structure* 3, no. 2 (1961): 49–51, here 49. Quoted in Jonneke Jobse, *De Stijl Continued: The Journal* Structure *(1958–1964); An Artists' Debate* (Rotterdam: 010 Publishers, 2005), 268.

90 Anthony Hill, "Programme. Paragram. Structure," in *Data: Directions in Art, Theory and Aesthetics*, ed. Anthony Hill (London: Faber & Faber, 1968), 251–69, here 263.

91 Hill, "Programme. Paragram. Structure," 262–63.

of the paintings have an effect separate from literal visual perception? Hill calls for a program of research—"a general phenomenology of structure"[92]—to work through these questions, and he wrote another essay, "Art and Mathesis: Mondrian's Structures," in which he floats the possibility of "establishing the '*set* of Mondrian's axioms'" in terms of graph theory.[93] A mathematical analysis of Mondrian's paintings proved to be more involved than even a dense academic paper could accommodate, however. According to Hill, "it would be necessary to examine around 130 of Mondrian's compositional schemes and to compute the topological information content of each scheme."[94]

Pursing this line of inquiry would amount to an ambitious research agenda for subjecting loose mathematical insights to rigorous questioning and precise experimentation. Hill believed he was taking the next step in the project of constructivism: to abandon artistry in favor of effects, to abandon intuition in favor of procedure, and to abandon the persona of the genius in favor of the scientist or laboratory technician.

---

92 Hill, "Programme. Paragram. Structure," 264.

93 Anthony Hill, "Art and Mathesis: Mondrian's Structures," *Leonardo* 1, no. 3 (July 1968): 233–42, 234.

94 Notice the similar call to comprehensiveness in Lévi-Strauss's proposal for computer-use in anthropology: Claude Lévi-Strauss, "The Structural Study of Myth," *Journal of American Folklore* 68, no. 270 (1955): 428–44, cf. 443.

FROM *CIRCLE* TO *DATA*: AVANT-GARDE ROUTINES

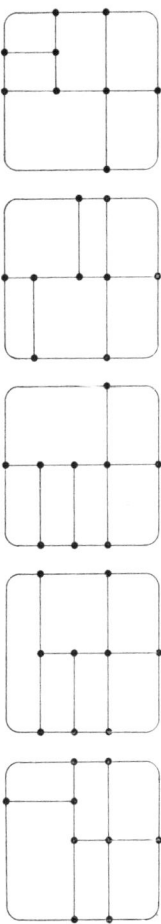

13 Anthony Hill, *Five Ways of Drawing the Identity Network of Composition with Red and Blue by Piet Mondrian*, 1968

STRUCTURALISM: THE FORM OF LANGUAGE

In generalizing from the Constructionist Group to the art and architecture scene of the 1960s writ large, it was not the discipline of mathematics *per se* that best characterized what was happening, but the way in which mathematics served as a common language, allowing a "channel of communication" between disciplines.[95]

But language here must be understood in a specific sense: the structuralist sense. An important clue comes in the final section of Hill's essay on Mondrian's structures when he mentions "Bourbaki's concept of structure."[96] Nicolas Bourbaki was the pseudonym under which a collective of mostly French mathematicians set out to reform their discipline beginning in the 1930s. The collective's epic book series, the *Éléments de mathématique*, "undertook the monumental task of reorganizing mathematics in terms of basic structural components."[97] The commonality between Mondrian's artistic project and Hill's research in graph theory was not any particular mathematical axiom or formula, but what Bourbaki called a "structural type."[98] It was this underlying structure that linked logical axioms, modes of investigation, and particular works of art or mathematical proofs. In place of the disciplinary differences that kept art and science at a respectful distance from one another (as in *Circle* in 1937), the Constructionists in 1968 worked within an intellectual framework that was shared across these boundaries. Orientation toward such a framework, language, or structure

---

95 The journal *Leonardo* was a product of the same thinking as *Data*; it was founded by Frank Malina in 1968 as "a channel of communication between artists" (that is, a foundation for a sustained collective research agenda) on the topic of "scientific techniques of possible use to artists." Frank J. Malina, "Aims and Scope of Leonardo," *Leonardo* 1, no. 1 (January 1968): 1–2. Malina will turn up again in this chapter regarding the journal *Image*. For a detailed account of connections between modern mathematics and architecture, see Theodora Vardouli, *Graph Vision: Digital Architecture's Skeletons*, forthcoming (Cambridge, MA: MIT Press, 2024).

96 Hill, "Art and Mathesis," 241.

97 Rene Thom, quoted in Leo Corry, *Modern Algebra and the Rise of Mathematical Structures*, 2nd ed. (Basel: Birkhäuser, 2004), 289.

98 Structural types include, e.g., algebraic structures, order structures, and topological structures. Hill, "Art and Mathesis," 241.

STRUCTURALISM: THE FORM OF LANGUAGE

was known in the 1960s as structuralism.[99] Just as Bourbaki was an exemplar of structuralist mathematics, the Constructionist Group exemplified structuralist art.

Structuralism grew into an epoch-defining intellectual phenomenon in 1950s Paris. Its broadest influence in the 1960s was to reframe the human sciences as "questionable sciences"; disciplines such as anthropology and psychology that operated at some remove from the rigors of mathematics were found to come up short when measured against the "hard sciences" in terms of precision and prestige.[100] The French anthropologist Claude Lévi-Strauss was the central figure in the early years of structuralism, both within his own discipline and as an example for others. Following fieldwork and teaching in São Paulo and New York, Lévi-Strauss returned to Paris and published his first major work in 1949, *Les Structures élémentaires de la parenté* (The elementary structures of kinship), which developed an approach that upended typical anthropological methods. His research program promised to bring universality to fields characterized by detailed regional studies. In "The Structural Study of Myth," for instance, Lévi-Strauss posed the question of global commonality that haunted studies of mythology: "If the content of a myth is contingent, how are we going to explain that throughout the world myths do resemble one another so much?"[101] Using charts and formulas to map out the elements of various myths and to understand their internal organization—and then to compare mythological systems developed in different parts of the world with one

---

99 For an overview of the rise of structuralism, see Francois Dosse, *History of Structuralism, vol 1: The Rising Sign, 1945–1966* (Minneapolis: University of Minnesota Press, 1997).

100 Michel Foucault was at the forefront of criticism of the changes underway. See, e.g., Michel Foucault, *The Order of Things: An Archaeology of Human Sciences*, trans. Alan Sheridan (New York: Pantheon, 1970). The term "questionable sciences" and its equation with the human sciences is from John Dupré, *Human Nature and the Limits of Science* (Oxford: Clarendon, 2001), 113.

101 Lévi-Strauss, "Structural Study of Myth," 429.

another—Lévi-Strauss comes to the conclusion that "every myth ... corresponds to a formula" of a certain type:

$$fx(a) : fy(b) \approx fx(b) : fa\text{-}1(y)^{102}$$

While this formula itself is questionable (we will return to it again below), the implications of Lévi-Strauss's method are striking. He concludes that there is no real difference between the most advanced European thinking and "the so-called 'primitive' mind": "The kind of logic which is used by mythical thought is as rigorous as that of modern science ... the difference lies not in the quality of the intellectual process, but in the nature of the things to which it is applied."[103] Many found this ecumenical approach appealing. By the end of the 1950s, investigations of epistemic structures (to use Michel Foucault's term) were happening everywhere, and structuralism was taken by many to be the best hope for leading the human sciences into a new golden age of legitimacy and relevance.[104]

The foundational insight of structuralism derives from the work of the Swiss linguist Ferdinand de Saussure. De Saussure's *Cours de linguistique générale* (Course in General Linguistics) of 1916 presented an alternative to the usual way language was being studied. Nineteenth-century linguistics, as de Saussure describes it, was dominated by philology: Linguists took a historical view, showing how the meanings of words change over time and how languages evolve.[105] Friedrich Nietzsche famously found this retrospective academic impulse deadening: "There is a degree of insomnia, of rumination, of historical sense which injures every living thing and finally destroys it, be it a man, a people or a culture."[106]

---

102 Lévi-Strauss, "Structural Study of Myth," 442.
103 Lévi-Strauss, "Structural Study of Myth," 444.
104 Foucault, *Order of Things*, xxii; Dosse, *History of Structuralism*, 173.
105 See Fredric Jameson, *The Prison-House of Language: A Critical Account of Structuralism and Russian Formalism* (Princeton: Princeton University Press, 1972).
106 Friedrich Nietzsche, *On the Advantage and Disadvantage of History for Life*, trans. Peter Preuss (Indianapolis: Hackett, 1980), 10.

De Saussure offered a radically different approach: studying the totality of a language at a given moment by focusing on rules of syntax and relationships between words. Meaning, then, was not to be found in the origin or evolution of words, but in the webs of linguistic / social relationships that constitute cultures.[107] The most important of de Saussure's axioms for modern linguistics was his idea that there are two complementary aspects of language: the linguistic structure (grammar and syntax), which members of a culture learn through enculturation and carry in their minds (for the most part unconsciously) as an abstract system; and the everyday, living, spoken aspect of language—language as it is concretely enacted.

De Saussure's two-sided concept of language—structure and expression—became the foundational conceptual icon of semiotics and then structuralism.[108] Anthropologists such as Lévi-Strauss expanded from specifically linguistic structures to the frameworks of collective life more broadly, which recast de Saussure's dichotomy as *social* structure and *cultural* expression. (Because cultural life occurs largely through the medium of language, this was not a difficult leap.) Structuralism brought about a disciplinary Gestalt shift in anthropology, from the details of commonplace cultural interactions to the big picture of social relations. Anthropologists hoped to understand the unifying code behind multifarious phenomena. Social structures and ways of life could be mapped and compared; historically situated content gave way to spatial and formal analyses; anthropology imagined becoming a science based on the mathematics of morphology and topology (fig. 14). The intellectual excitement was dizzying, and structuralism was applied with revolutionary fervor across academia.

---

[107] On "webs of significance," see Clifford Geertz, "Deep Play: Notes on the Balinese Cockfight," *Daedalus* 101, no. 1 (1972): 1–37. Regarding cultural studies, see Stuart Hall's influential book: Stuart Hall, ed., *Representation: Cultural Representations and Signifying Practices* (London: Sage, 1997).

[108] Dosse, *History of Structuralism*, 101.

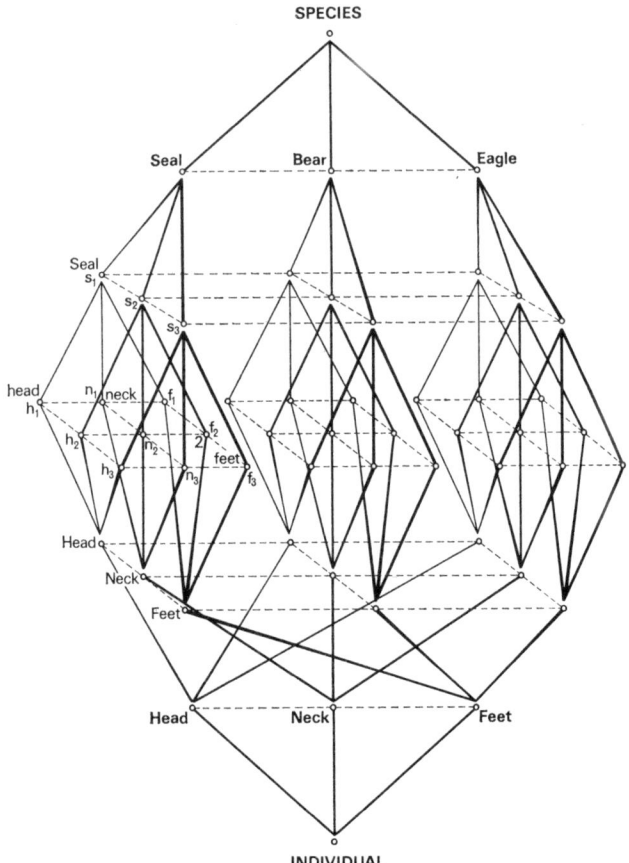

14 Claude Lévi-Strauss, "Totemic Operator," 1962

In each field it entered, structuralism was productive to the degree to which it was counterintuitive. The semiotician Algirdas Greimas explored relationships between signs and concepts through "semiotic squares" embodying logical calculi, an exploratory method later applied by art theorists and cultural critics such as Rosalind Krauss and Fredric Jameson to map field of possibilities, raising perplexing questions such as: What is both architecture and not-architecture? (fig. 15).[109] In lectures designed to provoke and confound, Jacques Lacan outlined elusive structures of the human mind; his "mathemes" fit our deepest desires into formulas that appear tidy but spin off vertiginously upon prodding (fig. 16).[110]

Lévi-Strauss reached the point in his study of indigenous mythological systems that it became a properly bureaucratic endeavor:

> It should be emphasized that the task of analyzing mythological literature, which is extremely bulky, and of breaking it down into its constituent units, requires team work and secretarial help. A variant of average length needs several hundred cards to be properly analyzed. To discover a suitable pattern of rows and columns for those cards, special devices are needed, consisting of vertical boards about two meters long and one and one-half meters high, where cards can be pigeon-holed and moved at will; in order to build up three-dimensional models enabling one to compare the variants, several such boards are necessary, and this in turn requires a spacious workshop, a kind of commodity particularly unavailable in Western Europe nowadays.[111]

---

[109] Rosalind Krauss, "Sculpture in the Expanded Field," *October* 8 (1979): 30–44. On the "semiotic square," see Jameson, *Prison-House of Language*, 163.

[110] Lacan presumably derived the term "matheme" from combining "mathematics" with Claude Lévi-Strauss's "mytheme" (relating to basic constituents of mythological systems).

[111] Lévi-Strauss, "Structural Study of Myth," 443.

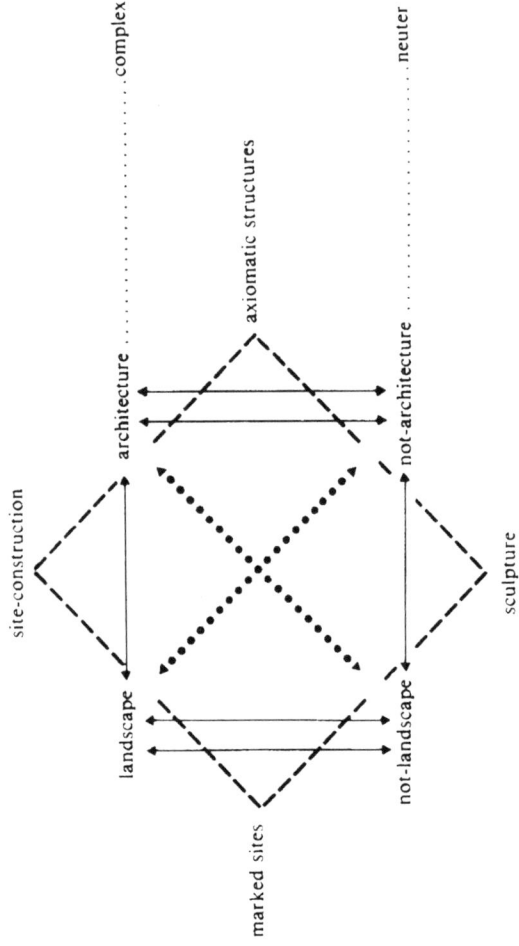

15 Rosalind Krauss, "Sculpture in the Expanded Field," 1979

STRUCTURALISM: THE FORM OF LANGUAGE

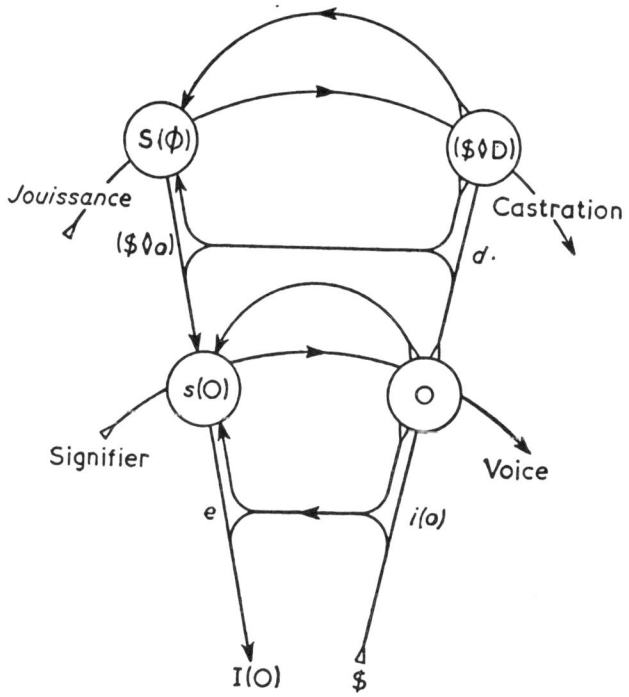

16 Jacques Lacan, "Graph of Desire," 1960

He goes on to lament that structuralist ethnographic analysis would soon "require I.B.M. equipment" to sort out. Lévi-Strauss gambled that the shock of new methods that placed computers alongside "primitive societies" would jumpstart a cycle of disciplinary change.

Such was the atmosphere in the highly competitive intellectual scene of 1950s Paris, and it spread. Lévi-Strauss's "The Structural Study of Myth" was translated into English in 1955, followed by *Structural Anthropology* and *Totemism* in 1963 and several more of his books in the following decade. By the mid-1970s, British theorists were reminiscing about the heyday of the structuralist "gang of four:" Lévi-Strauss, Lacan, Foucault, and Roland Barthes (the last of whom we will encounter in the next chapter).[112] In the meantime, in the mid- to late 1960s, one discipline after another was caught up in the intellectual passion for semiotic analysis. The year *Data* was published, 1968, can be considered the moment of peak structuralism in the English-speaking world.

Structuralism gave to art and architecture a fresh set of terms and techniques to fuel disciplinary agendas that were already underway. The Constructionist Group reformulated constructivist art in structuralist terms to make room for its members among established figures. Architecture was feeling its own disciplinary crisis, which Summerson persuasively diagnosed as the result of encroachments by other professions (engineering and planning[113]), changes in the distribution of labor within the building industry (the

---

112 See John Sturrock, *Structuralism and Since: From Lévi Strauss to Derrida* (Oxford: Oxford University Press, 1979). As another reference point, J. G. Merquior calls out Lévi-Strauss, Barthes, Derrida, Lacan, Althusser, and Foucault as top structuralists. Even through the 1980s, the line between structuralism and post-structuralism was blurry. See J.G. Merquior, *From Prague to Paris: A Critique of Structuralist and Post-Structuralist Thought* (London: Verso, 1986). For a helpful guide, see Gilles Deleuze, "How Do We Recognize Structuralism?," trans. Michael Taormina, in *Desert Islands, and Other Texts (1953–1974)*, ed. David Lapoujade (Los Angeles: Semiotext(e), 2004), 170–92.

113 Summerson, "TVA"; John Summerson, "London Re-Grouped," *The Listener* 755 (July 1943): 16.

rise of the architect-bureaucrat[114]), and a lack of guiding theoretical principles (which resulted in architecture's "missing language" problem[115]). While on the surface essays like Rowe's "Mathematics of the Ideal Villa" imply that architects were busily importing ideas from mathematics, what was happening would be more appropriately characterized as a sympathy of methods between a structuralist conception of mathematics and a structuralist conception of architecture. Structuralist theory served as a common framework that allowed ideas to be traded between disciplines.[116]

The material the Constructionist Group made use of was largely inherited from earlier abstract art, generally De Stijl and the Russian artistic movements now grouped under the title of constructivism. In architecture, the pervasive linguistic analogy of rationalism (which Summerson succinctly identified in *The Classical Language of Architecture*) guaranteed that architectural rules and elements—"languages"—would be available everywhere architects looked as they adopted a structuralist mindset. Summerson pointed to Le Corbusier's language of prismatic forms (fig. 17); Rowe outlined a language of proportion from Renaissance humanism; and the "classical language" of the orders or even the "language" of suburban domestic ornamentation would serve just as well (fig. 18).[117]

As with the concept of natural beauty, much of the effect of structuralist theory in architecture was derived from the way it conflated preexisting categories. For Summerson and other theorists since Claude Perrault, language was

---

114 Summerson, "Bread & Butter."

115 Summerson, "Case for a Theory."

116 On the useful concept of inter-disciplinary "trading zones," see Peter Galison, *Image and Logic: A Material Culture of Microphysics* (Chicago: University of Chicago Press, 1997), 783.

117 Rowe picked up the discourse on proportions from his teacher, Rudolf Wittkower. See, e.g., Anthony Vidler, *Histories of the Immediate Present: Constructing Architectural Modernism* (Cambridge, MA: MIT Press, 2008), 61–104.

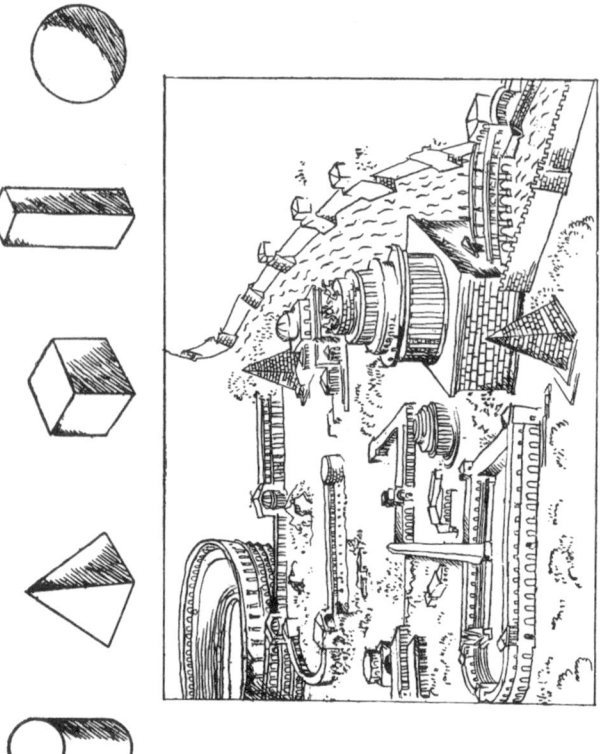

17 Le Corbusier, "Lesson of Rome," 1923

STRUCTURALISM: THE FORM OF LANGUAGE

18 Robert Venturi, Denise Scott Brown, and Steven Izenour, "Precedents of Suburban Symbols," 1970 (drawn by Robert Miller)

understood to be the realm of conventional meaning.[118] If Corinthian columns are appropriate for a capitol building and rustication is appropriate for a barracks, this was a matter of historical association bordering on the random. Language was understood as an evolving set of elements, each with their own contingent histories of meaning. The insight of structuralism was to argue that even a classical language could be analyzed in a modern way, as a structure of rules and relationships, just as a scientifically minded architect would approach any other formal system. Besides the *language of form*, structuralism insisted that architects pay attention to the *form of language*. Structuralism is a generalized formalism—a formalism of form, an abstraction of the abstract. From a structuralist point of view, the distinction between architectural programs and architectural forms, which Summerson found so difficult to reconcile (as outlined in the Prologue), tends to dissolve. Both are governed by deeper structure.

After a structuralist mindset was adopted and a set of elements chosen, there remained the task of working with them. This is where the computer—a structuralist device if there ever was one—enters our story. Here we must contend with the specter of determinism. Did the arrival of the computer *cause* architects to work in a certain way? An apt analogy can be found in the old saying that "if all you have is a hammer, everything looks like a nail." With computers at hand, architecture began to look like a matter of formal languages and structured data, and structuralist fantasies seeped into ever-wider habits of thought. Just as anthropologists and artists calibrated their agendas to the rigors of computation, architects would learn to dream computationally as well.[119]

---

118 Claude Perrault, *Ordonnance des cinq especes de colonnes selon la methode des anciens* (Paris: Jean Baptiste Coignard, 1683).

119 Against simplistic, one-way determinism (in which computers are imagined to have *caused* architects to work in a certain way), a deeper analysis can be achieved by seeing architecture and digital technologies as having been co-

produced within the same cultural milieu and as a result of ongoing conceptual exchange. See Antoine Picon, "Digital Technology and Architecture: Towards a Symmetrical Approach," *TAD* 6, no. 1 (2022): 10–14.

STRUCTURALIST ACTIVITY IN *FORM*

The journal *Form* consolidated structuralist tendencies in the British artistic scene and facilitated their spread into architecture. Unlike *Circle* or *Data*, *Form* was not only modeled on earlier avant-garde publications, but it was itself a true "little magazine," with ten issues appearing between 1966 and 1969.[120]

It was produced from within a particular artistic subculture: *Form*'s three editors met at the Society of Arts in Cambridge.[121] They were students at the University of Cambridge, where a center of experimentation in architectural science and computation, the Centre for Land Use and Built Form Studies, opened in 1967. This was a culmination of "the Cambridge phenomenon"; a heady mix of computation, philosophy, science, and design was palpably "in the air."[122]

Form's de facto editor in chief, Philip Steadman, was an architecture student at Cambridge who supplied the technical and organizational acumen.[123] The other two editors, Stephen Bann and Mike Weaver, brought much of the artistic raw material and structuralist theory from their perspectives as doctoral students in history and English.[124] As students rather than professional architects or artists, the three editors reached widely—almost randomly—into the most interesting corners of the surrounding artistic scene. One of their

---

120 For context, see R. J. Ellis, "Mapping the United Kingdom Little Magazine Field," in *New British Poetries: The Scope of the Possible*, ed. Robert Hampson and Peter Barry (Manchester: University of Manchester Press, 1993), 72–102. More generally, see Colomina, *Clip, Stamp, Fold*; Steven Heller, *Merz to Emigre and Beyond: Avant-Garde Magazine Design of the Twentieth Century* (London: Phaidon, 2003).

121 Joaquim Moreno, "Interview with Stephen Bann," in *Clip, Stamp, Fold: The Radical Architecture of Little Magazines, 196X to 197X*, ed. Beatriz Colomina (Barcelona: Actar, 2011), 223–24.

122 For context, see Mary Louise Lobsinger, "Two Cambridges: Models, Methods, Systems, and Expertise," in *A Second Modernism: MIT, Architecture, and the "Techno-Social" Moment*, ed. Arindam Dutta (Cambridge, MA: MIT Press, 2013), 652–85.

123 The editorial archive of *Form*, now at Princeton, shows Steadman to be the central organizing figure.

124 Gustavo Grandal Montero, "From Cambridge to Brighton: Concrete Poetry in Britain, an Interview with Stephen Bann," in *Artist's Book Yearbook 2016–2017* (Bristol: Impact Press, 2015), 70–93, here 71.

tasks in the Society of Arts was to invite artists to give talks in Cambridge, and they relished the contact with notoriety and avant-garde ideas. Guests included Victor Pasmore, the central figure of the Constructionist Group, and Larry Rivers, the "godfather of pop art." Various greats like Allen Ginsberg and Karlheinz Stockhausen also passed through Cambridge in the same years. Part of the fun of *Form* was to continue such engagement with cultural icons.[125] Contributions by Raoul Hausmann and Hans Richter from the established European avant-garde stand out as editorial coups that anchored an illustrious cast of characters over the journal's ten issues.[126] The editors' broad involvement with the artistic scene in and around London also led to a few elaborate events. In 1964 they pulled together the grandly titled *First International Exhibition of Concrete and Kinetic Poetry*, which included ninety-three works from Latin America and Europe as well as from local artists.[127] By the end of its three-year run, *Form* had become a focal point of the artistic avant-garde in Britain.[128]

A trial run of the project began when Steadman gained editorial control over a London-based arts magazine, *Image*, after having worked as its graphic designer.[129] The issues of *Image* from 1964 to 1966 thus served essentially as issues −2, −1, and 0 of *Form*. The enterprise began modestly, with a confusing mix of disconnected material from the previous editorial direction, but the final issue of *Image* was a coherent special issue on kinetic art and concrete poetry that remains a key document of the era. It included two essays by two

---

125 Author's interview with Philip Steadman, March 2017.

126 This was an impressive accomplishment for the journal's young and unknown editors. The correspondence in the *Form* archive shows the spectacularly successful results of Steadman's efforts to solicit work from various artists.

127 A list is in *Granta* 68, no. 1240 (28 November 1964).

128 The *Form* archive contains dozens of unsolicited contributions from British artists. When Steadman shut down the journal after its tenth issue, letters poured in mourning the community's loss.

129 Joaquim Moreno, "Interview with Philip Steadman," in *Clip, Stamp, Fold: The Radical Architecture of Little Magazines, 196X to 197X*, ed. Beatriz Colomina (Barcelona: Actar, 2011), 507–9.

of *Form*'s editors—Bann and Weaver—that are among the clearest theoretical statements on their subjects. Following a few other essays on the history and scope of current avant-garde artistic production and a thorough historical essay by Steadman on color music, the remaining bulk of the issue consisted of an array of examples of recent artistic experimentation.

The arts appear to have been flourishing. The issue includes several of the hanging mobiles and shape poems that are now most readily associated with kinetic art and concrete poetry, but there are also Plexiglas boxes with moving blotches of light (by Frank Malina, who founded the journal *Leonardo* three years later), works that look like paintings made of overlapping shards of colored glass (by Andree Dantu), text swirling in hallucinogenic graphic fields (by Sylvester Houédard), and an artist standing grinning in the desert beside a rocket ready to launch (again by Frank Malina).[130] Altogether, the final issue of *Image* presents contemporary artistic practice as a wide-ranging experimentation with forms, materials, and techniques.

The first issue of *Form* continues down parallel tracks of artistic production and theoretical elaboration, and the diversity is unabated. An essay by Theo van Doesburg written in 1929, "Film as Pure Form," leads the issue, setting the tone and ambition for what follows with a classic statement of De Stijl motivation: "The problem of film as an independent creative form has made no great progress in the last decade."[131] Van Doesburg elaborates a rather cryptic theory of space and its relationship to film, and he presents his own works

---

130 Malina was an aeronautical engineer and pioneer of rocketry as well as an artist and editor.

131 Theo van Doesburg, "Film as Pure Form," *Form* 1 (1966): 5–11, here 5. On the place of van Doesburg in architecture theory in this period, see Yve-Alain Bois, "Mondrian and the Theory of Architecture," *Assemblage* 4 (October 1987): 102–30. Van Doesburg's awkward phrasing is intended to emphasize that the medium of film is the locus of unresolved disciplinary "problems." Clement Greenberg famously took up this type of "medium specificity" analysis in the years around 1960. See Clement Greenberg, "Modernist Painting," *Arts Yearbook* 4 (1961): 101–8.

that study "elements" of film using various techniques.[132] The fact that *Form*'s editors found the essay worth reprinting four decades after it was written suggests that they thought that little progress had been made in the intervening years: It was time to once again tackle "the problem of film" (that is, the untapped disciplinary potential of the medium). And film was not the only creative form in need of revitalization. The following essays in the first issue discuss (in order of appearance): graphic design, International Style architecture, the paintings of Fernand Léger, computer-aided design, typography, historical avant-garde poetry, and recent concrete poetry.

Exploration of these forms and others continued in the following nine issues, but it was concrete poetry that was the most consistently theorized in the journal—and the theory of choice was structuralism. Though the term "concrete poetry" groups together a wide variety of practices in the 1960s British poetry scene,[133] it can be imagined as a practice of taking the raw material of poetry—words on a page, in one formulation—and expanding the field of possible things to be done with that raw material in every conceivable direction.

Poetry, generally, was of deep interest to the editors of *Form*. Bann had been winning medals for his poetry since childhood, and as an undergraduate student he had written for the literary journal *Granta* (the one poem he submitted, however, was rejected).[134] Weaver, for his part, was writing a dissertation on the modernist American poet William Carlos Williams. If poetry is approached as *words on a page*, one of the first expanded possibilities that suggests itself is to work with the page as a visual space. This sort of investigation was not new in the 1960s: Stéphane Mallarmé and Guillaume

---

132 For an insightful discussion, see Richard Difford, "Developed Space: Theo van Doesburg and the Chambre de Fleurs," *The Journal of Architecture* 12, no. 1 (2007): 79–98.

133 Bob Cobbing, *Changing Forms in English Visual Poetry: The Influence of Tools and Machines* (London: Writers Forum, 1988).

134 See Grandal Montero, "From Cambridge to Brighton," 73–75.

Apollinaire, for instance, had each worked with space and poetry in strikingly different ways in nineteenth- and early-twentieth-century Paris. And British concrete poets were well aware of this: The cover of the eighth issue of *Form* features a poem by Apollinaire (fig. 19).[135]

This consideration of novelty and precedents is crucial for understanding the ideas about art that motivated *Form*. On the whole, concrete poets were less interested in establishing an entirely new field than development and discovery within a preexisting field of possibilities. In the first issue of *Form*, a poem by Pedro Xisto places the words *star*, *astro*, *rats*, and *ostra* in the white expanse of the blank page, with a thin line running down the middle. The reader's eyes ping-pong between the words, spotting poetic implications in the process. The timeless vocation of poetry is not overthrown but reimagined to include new possibilities (such as relatively open spatial discovery). Near the end of the third issue of *Form* is a reprint of a poem by Kurt Schwitters, the German Dadaist provocateur. It is a sequence of capital consonants ("W W / PBD / ZFM / RF RF TZPF TZPF," etc.), below which is printed a "trial guide to pronunciation." Alongside the poem is an essay in which Schwitters argues that "the basic material of poetry is not the word but the letter."[136] Other concrete poets used rhythms of dictation as their basic material. A poem by Ian Hamilton Finlay in the final issue of *Image* presents three columns of words that can be read as sequences with different beats: The first column reads at a fast clip; the second offers a quick alternation of varying words; the third, a plodding sequence of heavy words. Sometimes the poetic structure was more elaborate. Elsewhere, for instance, Weaver analyzes a poem with a looping structure similar to Lévi-Strauss's universal formula for myth

---

135 See also R. P. Draper, "Concrete Poetry," *New Literary History* 2, no. 2 (1971): 329–40.

136 Kurt Schwitters, "Logically Consistent Poetry," *Form* 2 (September 1966): 28.

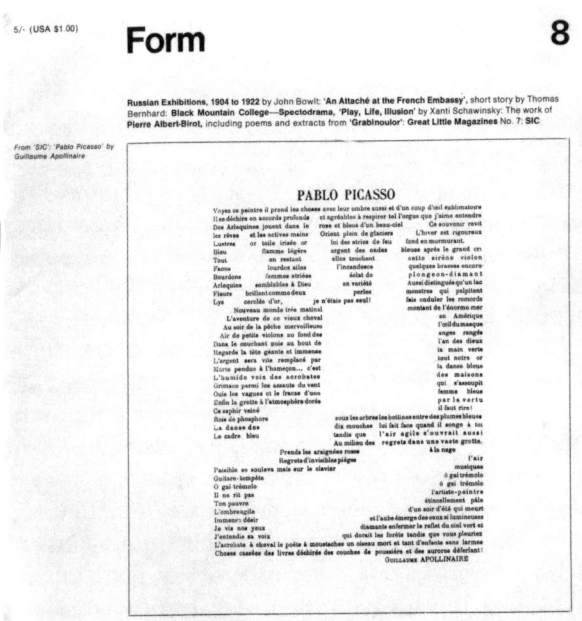

19 *Form* 8, 1968

(fig. 20).[137] These experiments construe poetry as a practice that deals not in the meanings of words but more broadly in perception and cognition.

Concrete poetry was one among many structuralist artistic practices in 1960s England, and the theoretical essays by Bann and Weaver in the final issue of *Image* apply to a much wider range than their ostensible subjects. Bann's essay on "communication and structure in concrete poetry" elaborates upon Ernst Gombrich's distinction between communication and expression in art. Against the vague (and popular) idea that artistic communication depends on "a kind of 'emotional contagion' between the artist and his public," Gombrich outlines a structuralist view.[138] In Bann's words, "Gombrich's theory … involves two positions—that a fixed vocabulary of conventional signs is necessary for communication in art and that the emotional weight of individual elements depends on their situation within a system of possibilities."[139] In Bann's interpretation, this means that artists work by setting up a "semantic space" in which they coordinate the reader's "exploration." Artistic practice is about striking a balance: deploying a "complex range of possibilities without overloading the expectations of the reader."[140]

In his concern for the mental impact of complexity, Bann was building on theories of cognition that were being developed in the 1960s.[141] In the end, Bann suggests that the goal of art is to produce flashes of insight: "Occasionally a

---

137 Mike Weaver, "Concrete Poetry," *Lugano Review* 1, no. 5 (1966): 100–125; cf. Lévi-Strauss, "Structural Study of Myth."

138 Stephen Bann, "Communication and Structure in Concrete Poetry," *Image*, Special issue, *Kinetic Art: Concrete Poetry* 1964, 8–9, here 8. See also page 217 of E.H. Gombrich and Ruth Shaw, "Symposium: Art and the Language of the Emotions," in *Proceedings of the Aristotelian Society, Supplementary*, vol. 36, 1962, 215–46.

139 Bann, "Communication and Structure," 8.

140 Bann, "Communication and Structure," 9.

141 See the introduction in Claudia Strauss and Naomi Quinn, *A Cognitive Theory of Cultural Meaning* (Cambridge: Cambridge University Press, 1997). See also chapter 1 in William M. Reddy, *The Navigation of Feeling: A Framework for the History of Emotions* (Cambridge: Cambridge University Press, 2001). For an example of widely read psychology on this topic from the era, see George Miller,

STRUCTURALIST ACTIVITY IN *FORM*

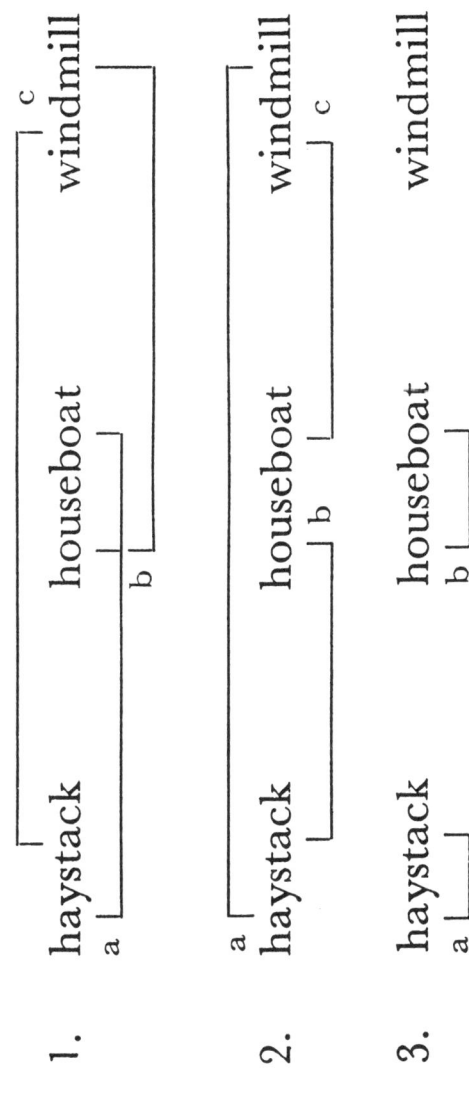

20 Mike Weaver, analysis of "Canal Stripe Series 3," 1966

poet will surprise us by discovering a new possibility" within "the structure of the work."[142] What Bann imagines is a cycle between a "normal science" of the arts and periodic innovation, to use the contemporary terms of Thomas Kuhn.[143] Bann ends with a quote from Gombrich that serves to contextualize the type of work that prevailed in *Form*: "What we call form in art, symmetries and simplicities of structure, might well be connected with the ease and pleasure of apprehension that goes with well-placed redundancies."[144] Generalizing from this, Bann suggests that the goal of concrete poetry—and, we might add, structuralist art more generally—is "for us to perceive the mysteries of structure at a conscious level."[145] (This is another way of pointing to the "general phenomenology of structure" that also fascinated Hill.)

In the tension between basic communication and mysterious meaning, however, structuralist art leans decisively toward the former. A characteristic anxiety of the editors of *Form* and many of its artists was the fear that, despite their efforts, nothing would be communicated at all. It is worth comparing concrete poetry in this regard to another formalist movement in poetry that flourished in Cambridge in the same period. A group associated with the British Poetry Revival was also located in the university town.[146] Jeremy Prynne, a leading figure in this group, published an essay in 1961 titled "Resistance and Difficulty," in which "he laid out a theory of the two qualities that would later become

---

"The Magical Number Seven plus or Minus Two: Some Limits on Our Capacity for Processing Information," *Psychological Review* 101, no. 2 (1955): 343–52.

142 Bann, "Communication and Structure," 9.

143 Thomas Kuhn, *The Structure of Scientific Revolutions* (Chicago: University of Chicago Press, 1962). Similar ideas were circulating in Cambridge in the work of Mary Hesse: Mary B. Hesse, *Models and Analogies in Science* (London: Sheed & Ward, 1963). See also Lionel March, "Introduction: The Logic of Design and the Question of Value," in *The Architecture of Form*, ed. Lionel March (Cambridge: Cambridge University Press, 1976), 1–40.

144 Gombrich and Shaw, "Symposium," 226.

145 Bann, "Communication and Structure," 9.

146 See Robert Sheppard, *The Poetry of Saying: British Poetry and Its Discontents, 1950–2000* (Liverpool: Liverpool University Press, 2005).

the dominant characteristics of his poetry."[147] The sort of poetic resistance and difficulty Prynne advocated is not hard to imagine; generally, it consisted of obscure word associations and complicated metrical qualities that only erudite formalist poets like himself would be equipped to appreciate.[148] It was in this larger context of British poetry that concrete poets shifted their focus to the everyday perception of relatively uninformed audiences. Weaver, in his theoretical statement, discussed a possible lowest common denominator for poetry:

> All that is asked of the perceiver (the former "reader") is that he should possess unimpaired sensory organs and an undamaged brain; a capacity for fantasy, or self-stimulation of the notoriously "literary" kind, is not required. To participate in the concrete poem means no more (no less) than paying active attention in perceiving. Theo Van Doesburg wrote, "in matters of art, comprehension is always impossible; as soon as it is comprehended, art ceases to be art."[149]

This shift from close reading to sensory perception served to move poetry into the realm of architecture—but only once architecture had been reimagined in terms of environmental effects. This was a reconceptualization that had long been in the works; it was a tenet of Neoplasticism, for example, as we encountered above in Mondrian's statement in *Circle*. The conflation of poetry and architecture can be seen most clearly in the fourth issue of *Form*, which documents the Brighton Festival Exhibition of Concrete Poetry.

---

147 Emily Witt, "That Room in Cambridge," *n+1* 11 (2011): 73–98, here 77.
148 "The difficulties this poetry poses for readers are potentially daunting. Complex hierarchies of syntactical dependence have to be followed and retraced, highly condensed and thoroughly dislocated references to the social world and its myriad discursive fields have to be followed up — and all the while readers' efforts are sabotaged by bathetic collapses, pratfalls, and aggression." Sam Ladkin and Robin Purves, "An Introduction," *Chicago Review* 53, no. 1 (2007): 6–13, here 10.
149 Weaver, "Concrete Poetry," 101.

Organized as an even more ambitious follow-up to the First International Exhibition, the Brighton Exhibition was scattered across an entire town, and it used urban elements as the medium of poetry. Edwin Morgan produced a set of "Festive Permutational Poems" that were placed in public buses, mimicking advertisements. This was kinetic art as well as concrete poetry: The ambulation of the buses supplied the permutational shuffling.[150] Claus Bremer installed a poem in the form of a banner above a park bench, and behind it Ian Hamilton Finlay arrayed a poem consisting of ampersands across a yard, turning the grass into a "page" and enacting a desire for radical inclusivity in the artform: People and things standing in the grass among the ampersands would complete the poem.

The resources of graphic design and advertising were fair game in the communication practices of concrete poets. A celebrated example is Décio Pignatari's 1957 poem, "Beba Coca Cola" (translated as "Drink Coca Cola"), which transforms its catchy title through a variety of immediately understandable permutations to arrive, in the end, at an opposite and equally blunt slogan: *cloaca* (sewer).[151] Besides slogans, the symbols and logos of consumer culture sometimes made their way into poems, particularly those of Brazilian poets who felt a pressure to set aside Portuguese in order to engage with the hegemonic American / global culture.[152] Closer to Cambridge, at the Brighton Exhibition, Kenelm Cox set up a poem consisting of three words—BEAUTY, LOVE, PASSION—buoyed above the water a short distance out into the ocean. A photograph with a small boat in the foreground captures the intention perfectly: the words of the poem use the same graphic material as the symbols and numbers on the boat's sail, and they happily

---

150 Grandal Montero, "From Cambridge to Brighton," 87.

151 See Jamie Hilder, *Designed Words for a Designed World: The International Concrete Poetry Movement, 1955–1971* (Montreal: McGill-Queen's University Press, 2016).

152 Hilder, *Designed Words*, 63.

21 Kenelm Cox, *Three Graces*, 1967

coexist in the same visual field (fig. 21). Poetry becomes environment, environment becomes poetry, and both merge into the architecture of everyday life.

In a more constrained form, Steadman helped produce Augusto de Campos's "cubepoem," wrapping thick Helvetica text around four brightly colored, collapsible panels (which, significantly, were in the same dimensions as *Form*).[153] This poem could be carried around and set up anywhere to stage an environmental intervention. It is reminiscent of the simple forms, bright colors, and bold graphics of Herbert Bayer's Bauhaus-era designs for cinemas and newspaper stands, the graphics of which were meant to cut through a cluttered visual environment to deliver their message (fig. 22).[154] The cover of the final issue of *Form* features a project by Alexander Rodchenko from 1923 that illustrates the underlying impulse. It is a project for a "cine-car," rendered using the bold simplicity of advertising graphics to communicate the revolution to the masses—and even going so far as to drive it to them and project it onto the sides of their buildings (fig. 23).

One insight that emerged from the concrete poetry scene before finding wider application was the idea that artistic techniques are more important than the materials being worked with. Any material could serve the structuralist artist. Poetry, graphic design, and architecture were construed as fundamentally the same thing, united by a common structure and common techniques. A clear statement of this approach is found in the first issue of *Form*, in an essay by the literary theorist Roland Barthes on "the activity of structuralism." The essay, which was translated from French for the

---

[153] Design iterations can be found in the *Form* archive. Helvetica was a rare and difficult font to use in Britain at the time. See Moreno, "Interview with Philip Steadman," 508. Steadman imagined at one point that *Form* would be published until a stack of them formed a cube. Author's interview with Philip Steadman, March 2017.

[154] See Ute Brüning, "Herbert Bayer," in *Bauhaus*, ed. Jeannine Fiedler and Peter Feierabend (Cologne: Könemann, 2000), 332–41.

STRUCTURALIST ACTIVITY IN *FORM*

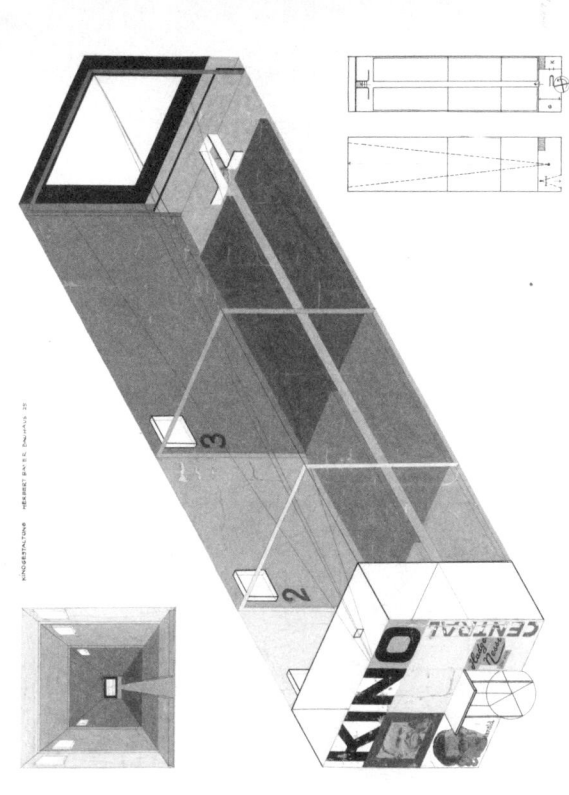

22 Herbert Bayer, "Design for a Cinema," 1924–25

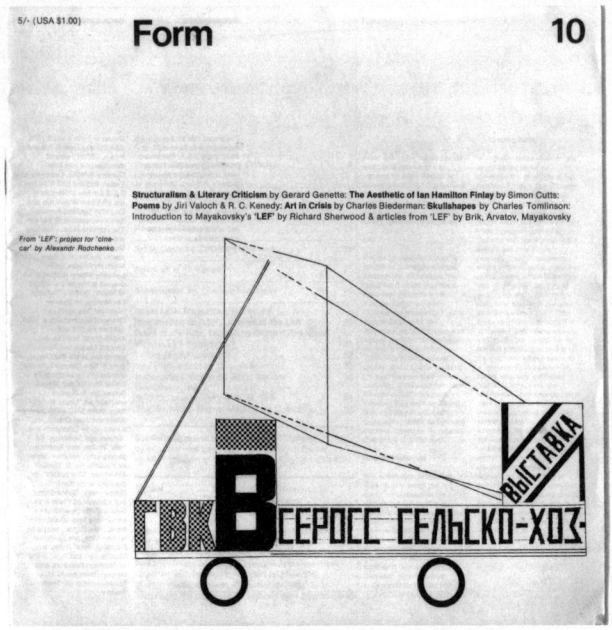

23 Form 10, 1969

first time for *Form,* serves as a manifesto for the structuralist artistic theory that underwrote the journal. Barthes puts it bluntly: "Technique is the very essence of all creation," he says—not ideas, not meaning, but *technique.*[155] This was a statement bordering on the outrageous in the context of French literature. He likely had the Oulipo group in mind (an abbreviation of Ouvroir de littérature potentielle, translated as "workshop of potential literature")—a group of writers and mathematicians whose work involved the formulation and excruciating application of rules.[156] (Georges Perec, for example, wrote a three-hundred-page novel, *La disparition*, without using the letter "e.") Barthes explains that structuralists do not create artworks but rather dissect some material and arrange it in a different way. In a definition similar to the one offered by Gombrich, Barthes says that "it is through the regular return of units and associations of units that the work appears to have been constructed, that is to say, endowed with meaning; the linguists call these rules of combination *forms.*"[157] Structuralist activity, then, leads to the construction of forms. Rather than forcing a choice between form and function, Barthes describes forms as functional units, and—looping back around—implies that function is generally about "fabricating meaning": Meaning, as Barthes describes it, is not something that exists inside the artwork to be transmitted to a passive spectator, but something the reader "fabricates" in her own mind. Agency is thus transferred from the artist to the reader—both engage in the same structuralist activity. The structuralist artist-technician constructs a machine for the reader to use to construct meaning, piece by piece, in a half-controlled manner, inside her own head. What sets Barthes's theoretical categories apart from one another is difficult to decipher, but at a practical level

---

155 Roland Barthes, "The Activity of Structuralism," trans. Stephen Bann, *Form* 1 (1966): 12–13.

156 See Alison James, *Constraining Chance: Georges Perec and the Oulipo* (Evanston: Northwestern University Press, 2009).

157 Barthes, "The Activity of Structuralism," 13.

his message is clear: Artists, the creators of lofty ideas, are out; technicians, who are inclined to tinker with the materials and effects of everyday life, are in.[158]

Barthes's manifesto imparts new value to one sort of technician in particular: the graphic designer. Throughout the pages of *Form*, we see graphic design as the technique held in common between architects, poets, painters, filmmakers, and practically everyone else. Steadman, the motivating force behind *Form*, produced few theoretical statements of his own, but instead carried out a torrent of "structuralist activity" in the guise of editing, typography, graphic design, and less glamorous writing (summaries, captions, and the like).[159] In *Image*, this came together as a bricolage—some incongruous paintings at the beginning followed by a strange advertisement / statement (or poem?) by a production company, the editorial located awkwardly in the middle of the issue, and a lot of concrete poetry and kinetic art making up the remaining bulk. Using his full editorial control of *Form*, Steadman engaged in a more holistic design effort. The journal was produced in an unusual square format, using Helvetica throughout.[160] Advertisements were absent (in the first issues at least). The format of the table of contents—epitomizing contemporary modernist layout techniques—appears to have been lifted from *Studio International*. A rigorous but flexible grid system ruled the remaining pages, with text and images often chopped and squished into place (fig. 24).

---

158 Barthes typically throws together similar terms in radical contradiction and in rapid succession: Structuralism, he says, "seeks to relate to history not simply contents (a thing which has been done a thousand times), but also forms, not simply the material, but also the intelligible, not simply the ideological but also the aesthetic." Barthes, "The Activity of Structuralism," 13. The precise meaning of this is nearly impossible to untangle—which is of course the point.

159 This is evident in the *Form* archive in the correspondence with authors—particularly the poets and artists—and the paste-up work of creating the journal's pages. One poet congratulated Steadman on the way his layout suited his concrete poems. Grandal Montero, "From Cambridge to Brighton," 224.

160 The journal was not much easier for the editors to produce than was *Circle* thirty years earlier. Moreno, "Interview with Philip Steadman," 504.

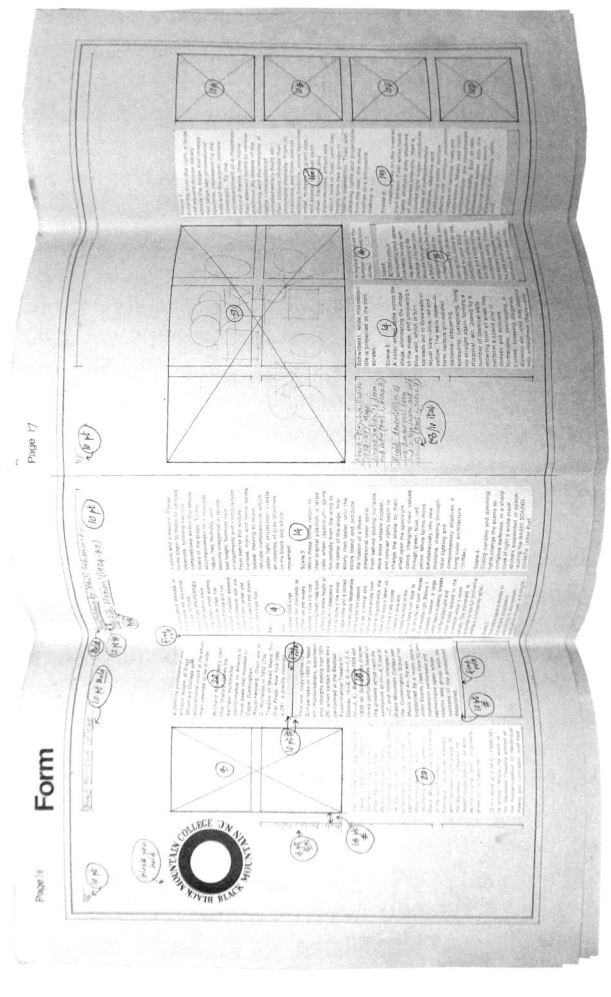

24 Paste-up of *Form*

The resulting design of *Form* pushed the agenda of "unification" inherited from the earlier British avant-garde (e.g., *Circle*) to its limit. Indeed, regular text is sometimes indistinguishable from poetry. The editors went to great lengths to find works that fit their mold, or could be made to fit.[161] Poems were generally redesigned in Helvetica, and resolutely idiosyncratic compositions like those of Sylvester Houédard (a respected father figure of British concrete poetry) were left out entirely. In its singularity of vision, *Form* stands in striking contrast to otherwise similar little magazines. Ian Hamilton Finlay's *Poor. Old. Tired. Horse.*, for example, drastically changed its layout and typography with each issue to suit its content.[162] The rigor of *Form* is likely attributable in part to the mindset Steadman had picked up as an architecture student under Leslie Martin, the architect and editor of *Circle* who was the director of the school of architecture at Cambridge from 1956.[163] But whatever its provenance—and its inspirations were surely multiple—*Form* is a clear embodiment of structuralist activity. Following Barthes, the graphic designer supersedes the artist and the architect, and the journal itself becomes a structuralist assemblage occupying the place once held by individual artworks.

Interpreting *Form* in the terms of the architectural theory of the preceding decades is revealing. Following Colin Rowe and Henry-Russell Hitchcock, Steadman's work on *Form* presents an investigation into "natural beauty" in the mode of the "bureaucrat"—a direction which, as we have seen in the case of the Constructionist Group, had been gaining momentum in Britain for two decades.[164] An urge toward anonymity pervades the journal. In his theoretical statement,

---

161 Fiery correspondence between Steadman and cantankerous poets is commonplace in the *Form* archive, as are thoughtful exchanges among the three editors.

162 All issues of the visual poetry magazine *Poor. Old. Tired. Horse.* (1962–1968) are available on UbuWeb at https://ubu.com/vp/Poor.Old.Tired.Horse.html.

163 Author's interview with Philip Steadman, March 2017.

164 Henry-Russell Hitchcock, "The Architecture of Bureaucracy and the

Weaver cites Jean Arp's wartime manifesto, "Abstract Art, Concrete Art":

> The works of concrete [art] must not bear the signature of their author. These paintings, these sculptures—these things—should be as anonymous in the great workshop of nature as clouds, mountains, seas, animals, and men. Yes—men too should become part of nature.[165]

Arp's polemic resonated in the atmosphere of postwar reconstruction. As he described it, form is something found, not created. Weaver summarizes nicely: "Concrete [art] is concerned with the discovery of form, the discovery of what Finlay calls 'an order *there*, somewhere, and not an order we can use (to save us, as it were) but more, that could use us.'"[166]

The activities channeled through *Form* are altogether less polemical than was typical of earlier modernist avant-garde production—no grand projects, no expansive urban interventions—but there is certainly a sense of a powerful force (the force of "nature") lurking behind their work.[167] Structuralist activity thus sometimes comes across as a voluntary submission to the force of form for access to its power over

---

Architecture of Genius," *Architectural Review* 101, no. 601 (January 1947): 3–6; Rowe, "Mathematics of the Ideal Villa."

165 Jean Arp, "Abstract Art, Concrete Art," in *Art of This Century: Objects, Drawings, Photographs, Paintings, Sculptures, Collages, 1910 to 1942*, ed. Peggy Guggenheim (New York: Art of This Century, 1942), 29–31. Quoted in Mike Weaver, "Concrete and Kinetic: The Poem as Functional Object," *Image*, Special issue, *Kinetic Art: Concrete Poetry* 1964, 14–15.

166 Weaver, "Concrete and Kinetic," 15.

167 For one polemical manifestation, see Lionel March, Marcial Echenique, and Peter Dickens, "Models of Environment: Polemic for a Structural Revolution," *Architectural Design* 41 (May 1971): 275. Generally, the artistic scene under discussion was notable for its even-keeled (even dryly historical) perspective. See, e.g., Hill, "Constructivism." None reaches anywhere near the level of Filippo Tommaso Marinetti's "Manifesto of Futurism": "Take up your pickaxes, your axes and hammers and wreck, wreck the venerable cities, pitilessly!" *Exhibition of Works by the Italian Futurist Painters* (London: Sackville Gallery, 1912), 6.

life. This ominous implication of management and control would soon render structuralism unpalatable to developing tastes.[168]

Although it evidently matched the contours of its era, it is important to understand one final conceptual development before the structuralist activity of *Form* can be seen to fit with computation in particular. If the artist is to become a technician, the artwork must become a machine—or perhaps a computational device. "Techniques" (of the artist) and "effects" (of the artwork) go together in *Form*. In the first essay in the first issue, van Doesburg presents the projector as an archetypal device for producing visual effects. László Moholy-Nagy's *Light Space Modulator*, which is featured in the sixth issue, represents the apotheosis of this ambition: It projects dynamic, multicolor light compositions onto every surface of the room around it, replacing the bland white walls of architecture with environmental effects (see fig. 5).[169]

This approach could easily be scaled up to the size of a small building: Issue five presents a project by Bernard Lassus for an inhabitable space around which "a complex reflecting surface is distorted continuously by the action of rods from above; rotating cylinders of different colours, at floor level, are illuminated from the side, and mirrored in the surface above."[170] Beyond such literal examples, any artistic medium could be thought of as an abstract machine—the artist needs only to specify the medium's properties and to figure out their associated techniques and effects.[171] If painting is about color on surfaces, an artist could add the element of time and put together a machine for producing "reflected light compositions." Or if music is about rhythms, the same

---

168 For a revealing case study, see Luke Skrebowski, "All Systems Go: Recovering Hans Haacke's Systems Art," *Grey Room* 30 (2008): 54–83.

169 See Istvan Kovacs, "Totality through Light: The Work of Laszlo Moholy-Nagy," *Form* 6 (December 1967): 14–19.

170 Bernard Lassus, "Environments and Total Landscape," *Form* 5 (September 1967): 13–15, here 14.

171 On the idea of "medium specificity," see Greenberg, "Modernist Painting."

machine could be used to make "color music." Steadman wrote an essay about Lumia, which did the latter, and the second issue of *Form* featured the work of the Bauhaus instructor Ludwig Hirschfeld-Mack, who did the former (fig. 25).[172]

In this effort to analyze, update, and systematize earlier directions in modern art, however, the notion of creating singular, elaborate machines to produce specific effects was beginning, by the mid-1960s, to appear obsolete.[173] A new class of general-purpose "hardware" was now available. In a long essay on color music, Steadman suggests that problems of "randomness of effect" and limitations to "basic composition" could be overcome by new computer technology:

> The use of some techniques which are currently being investigated experimentally—the generation of images electronically using cathode-ray tubes or electroluminescent display panels—may offer to the artist control over mobile forms in colour, and the possibility of rhythmic and "melodic" compositions perceived visually, of which the colour-musician has dreamed.[174]

Steadman later described his unrealized ambition of making elaborate color music compositions using a computer.[175] This possibility would have been obvious to any concrete poet who had seen the technology, but not many had. In the computers of the 1960s, the cathode-ray tube was certainly the most important piece of hardware for the artist, but it

---

[172] Basil Gilbert, "The Reflected Light Compositions of Ludwig Hirschfeld-Mack," *Form* 2 (1966): 10–13.

[173] One sign of the times was that machine metaphors were being replaced by systems metaphors. See, e.g., Eve Meltzer, *Systems We Have Loved: Conceptual Art, Affect, and the Antihumanist Turn* (Chicago: University of Chicago Press, 2013); Andreas Broeckmann, *Machine Art in the Twentieth Century* (Cambridge, MA: MIT Press, 2016).

[174] Philip Steadman, "Colour Music," in *Kinetic Art: Four Essays*, ed. Stephen Bann et al. (St. Albans: Motion Books, 1966), 16–25, here 24.

[175] Author's interview with Philip Steadman, March 2017.

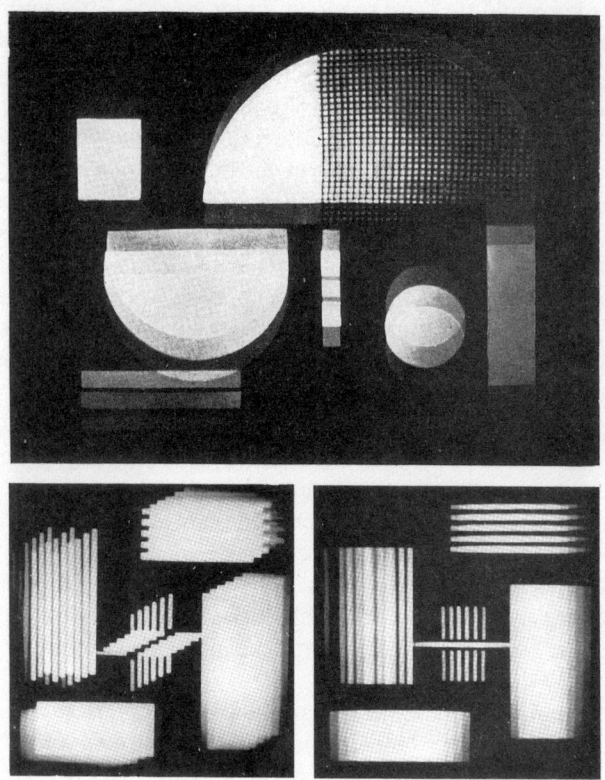

25 Ludwig Hirschfeld-Mack, reflected light compositions, c. 1923

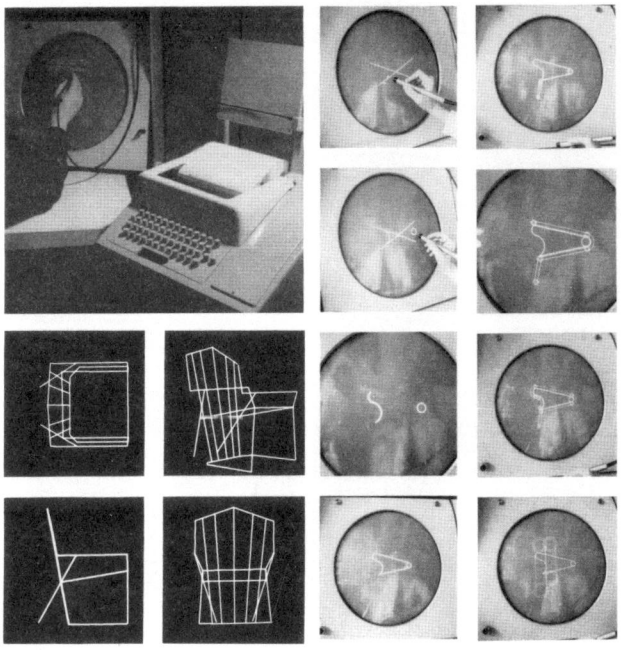

26 Computer-aided design demonstrations in *Form* 1, 1966

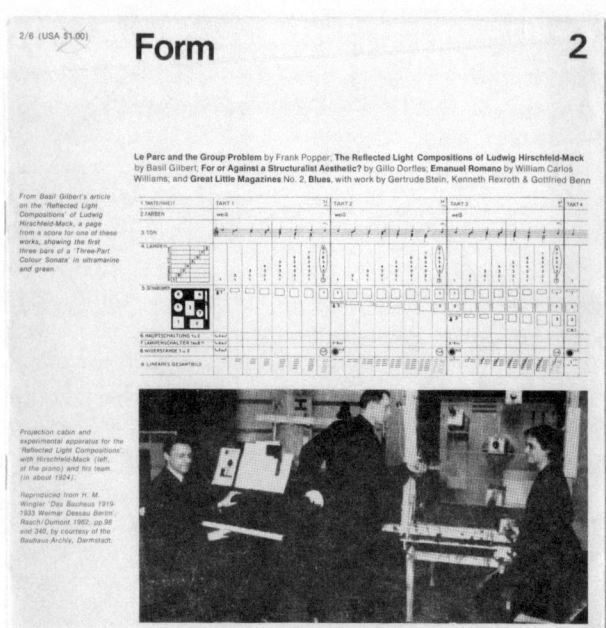

27 Form 2, 1966

was also the least known. The prevailing public imaginary of the computer was of giant "electronic brains," not windows onto interactive environments.[176] But Steadman and his colleagues at Cambridge were ahead of their contemporaries in this regard. Ivan Sutherland's famous demonstration of a proof-of-concept of general-purpose human–computer interactivity using screens and light pens took place at MIT in 1962, and three years later Sutherland was invited to present his work at Cambridge.[177] A write-up on Sketchpad and its implications for design using computers was published in the first issue of *Form*, in 1966.[178] The text is bland in comparison to the essays by van Doesburg and Barthes that it followed, but the images resonated powerfully: After a polemic about film and a theory of structuralist techniques and before a series of concrete poems, here was a technician pointing a light pen at a glowing screen to create what was essentially a work of kinetic art (fig. 26). Computer-aided design combined a device with a procedure that could be applied to any artform—a meta-medium to encompass all creative media.[179] The score of a reflected light composition on the cover of the second issue of *Form* appears to be, in

---

176 See Paul N. Edwards, *The Closed World: Computers and the Politics of Discourse in Cold War America* (Cambridge, MA: MIT Press, 1996). Christopher Alexander, an early computer-using architect, was adamant that computers were nothing but calculating machines. See Christopher Alexander, "A Much Asked Question about Computers and Design," in *Architecture and the Computer: Proceedings of the First Boston Architectural Center Conference* (Boston: Boston Architectural Center, 1964), 52–54. See also Alise Upitis, "Nature Normative: The Design Methods Movement, 1944–1967," PhD thesis (Massachusetts Institute of Technology, 2008); Matthew Allen, "Representing Computer-Aided Design: Screenshots and the Interactive Computer circa 1960," *Perspectives on Science* 24, no. 6 (2016): 637–68.

177 See Daniel Cardoso Llach, *Builders of the Vision: Software and the Imagination of Design* (London: Routledge, 2015); Philip Steadman, "Research in Architecture and Urban Studies at Cambridge in the 1960s and 1970s: What Really Happened," *Journal of Architecture* 21, no. 2 (February 2016): 291–306.

178 Crispin Gray, "Computers and Design," *Form* 1 (1966): 19–22.

179 On the dream of meta-media, see Lev Manovich, *Software Takes Command* (New York: Bloomsbury Academic, 2013). On the history of the media concept, see John Guillory, "Genesis of the Media Concept," *Critical Inquiry* 36 (2010): 321–62.

this context, essentially a computer program for the creation of architectural effects (fig. 27).

In the story of how a culture of computation developed within architecture, computer hardware was little more than a convenient vehicle for a generation to realize ambitions they inherited from avant-garde modernism and updated to match contemporary concerns. In *Form* we see all the strands come together: a model of artistic production (using a device or machine as a medium for the production of perceptual effects), an artistic medium (the interactive computer), a technique (procedurality), a figure who can carry out the work (the artist-technician), and the backing of theory (van Doesburg, Barthes, and many others). This was a sociotechnical assemblage that could be—and would be—applied anywhere and everywhere. It was the beginning of experimentation, not its end nor even its culmination.

One final strand should be added, although it stands somewhat apart from the others as a general tenet of modernism: a developmental understanding of art. The third essay in the first issue of *Form*, directly following van Doesburg and Barthes, is an essay on "experimental aesthetics" that describes how to evaluate the structuralist activity that follows. The advice is simple: Create a controlled environment and test artistic techniques in the same way that psychologists test perception.[180] Although this method—the scientific method—was rarely followed, it was the final conceptual step in the bureaucratization of aesthetics: Through controlled experimentation, an artistic agenda could become a research agenda. From discovery through production and into evaluation, art and architecture could be both programmed and made programmatic. They could be taken out of the hands of the artistic genius and given over to the structuralist technician.

---

180 Carolyn Cumming, "Experimental Aesthetics," *Form* 1 (1966): 14–15.

MOTIVATING THE ALGORITHM

It has been said that there are two ways to tell the history of computation.[181] In one view, computers are seen as calculating machines. Late-nineteenth- and early-twentieth-century business management looms large in this case, and the programmable electronic computer emerges as equipment to speed up calculation tasks like the census and payroll processing. The IBM mainframes of the 1950s fit within the corporate hierarchies of their era in a similar way to tabulating machines within the businesses of earlier times.[182] In the second view, computers are understood as devices for implementing algorithms, and they are placed within a history of mathematics and logic. Charles Babbage's Difference Engine (1830) thus appears similar to Gottfried Leibniz's Stepped Reckoner (1672) and Konrad Zuse's Z1 (1937), and the computer is seen as an instrument for solving mathematical problems.[183] Arguably, this mathematical lineage of computation eventually became a branch of knowledge: algorithmics.[184]

Hardware vs. software, business practices vs. mathematical concepts: Each of these ways of approaching the history of computation is relevant to architecture, as they are to most aspects of contemporary life. For the present account, however, it is worth elaborating the concept of the algorithm on its own to be sure it will not be lost in the practical history of computation-as-management.[185]

---

181 See Edwards, *Closed World*; Michael S. Mahoney, "The History of Computing in the History of Technology," *Annals of the History of Computing* 10, no. 2 (June 1988): 113–25.

182 For a longer view, see James R. Beniger, *The Control Revolution: Technological and Economic Origins of the Information Society* (Cambridge, MA: Harvard University Press, 1986).

183 See Jan von Plato, *The Great Formal Machinery Works: Theories of Deduction and Computation at the Origins of the Digital Age* (Princeton: Princeton University Press, 2017).

184 See Nicola Angius, Giuseppe Primiero, and Raymond Turner, "The Philosophy of Computer Science," in *The Stanford Encyclopedia of Philosophy*, ed. Edward N. Zalta (Metaphysics Research Lab, Stanford University, 2021), https://plato.stanford.edu/archives/spr2021/entries/computer-science/.

185 If computation is seen as "merely a tool," there is a danger that it will appear as if the introduction of computers into a field made no historical difference

At a basic conceptual level an algorithm is just a list of instructions, so we might expect to find them everywhere we look.[186] But it turns out to be unusual to find algorithms—that is, actual lists of instructions—even in disciplines with an element of procedurality. All sorts of activities are done one step at a time, to be sure, but it is rarely necessary to write these steps down. Here it helps to distinguish algorithms from related things. Looking at the explorations of mathematics by the Constructionist Group in *Data*, we find graphs and formulas but no algorithms. Likewise with the work of Lévi-Strauss, Lacan, and other (post-)structuralists: Mathematical exploration rarely became formal algorithmics. Most fields have historically found little use for explicitly formulated algorithms and associated methods of computation.

In a few fields, however, algorithmics became an important addition to existing disciplinary repertoires. An algorithm, unlike a formula, brings to the fore issues of managing relatively complex operations or sequences of effects—usually at a distance and executed by someone other than the person who wrote the algorithm. If a formula is like a single sentence, the totality of which can be easily held in the reader's mind, an algorithm is a longer text—perhaps a poem—in which a more elaborate structure involving something like a narrative arc or a complex framework of argumentation helps manage the reader's thoughts along the way.

Concrete poetry, as we encountered it in the previous chapter, is a field that is implicitly algorithmic: The poem is treated as a program to be run on the "hardware" of the human brain.[187] The structure of a concrete poem, however,

---

at all. See, e.g., Jon Agar, "What Difference Did Computers Make?," *Social Studies of Science* 36, no. 6 (December 2006): 869–907. For a critique of Agar, see Allen, "Representing Computer-Aided Design."

186 See Jean-Luc Chabert, ed., *A History of Algorithms: From the Pebble to the Microchip* (Berlin: Springer, 1999).

187 Thinking of the brain as a calculating machine was typical of the early years of computation. See Edwards, *Closed World*.

is not always a simple line-by-line sequence. Concrete poets often use the space of the page in a non-linear way, and it is hard to predict how a reader will navigate this multidimensional space. In an extended theoretical treatment of concrete poetry, Weaver (one of the editors of *Form*) described three types of concrete poems, two of which are algorithmic: "The optic or visual poet offers the poem as a constellation in space; the kinetic poet offers it as a visual succession; the phonetic poet offers it as an auditory succession."[188] "Visual successions" and "auditory successions" are algorithms. Weaver offers the example of Ernst Jandl's "Ode auf N," which presents a succession of "distorted versions of the word Napoleon" (e.g., "nanananana / naaaaaaaaaaa / poleoooon").[189] At no point is the full name pronounced, and indeed "the 'meaning' of the poem is not localized at one particular point in time." Rather, the poem presents a demonstration of how "the ear tries to make words out of syllables." The poem is an exercise in managing perception—for example, producing "the disgust in the rising intensity of *naaa*, held at the level *naaaaaaaaaaaa* to produce a sense of crisis and impending solution." In other poems, this sort of step-by-step management of perception takes the form of more complex mental movements, as with the looping steps of Finlay's *Canal Stripe Series 3* (see fig. 20).

In these and other cases, concrete poetry turns reading into an algorithmic exercise, and the concept of poetry is transformed in the process. As Weaver explains, "serial method replaces discursive grammar" and, ultimately, "the experimental emphasis falls on the micro-aesthetic of perception rather than on the macro-aesthetic of attitude. Energy is directed towards solving problems of scale, movement, sequential relations, time, stamina, and, above all, the identification of forms."[190]

---

188 Weaver, "Concrete Poetry," 100.
189 Weaver, "Concrete Poetry," 108.
190 Weaver, "Concrete Poetry," 100.

Similar algorithmic investigations took place in other artistic fields as well. Formalist literature after the Second World War, for example, often focused on such "serial methods" and "micro-aesthetics of perception."[191] The imperative of research and specialization in the university system of the Cold War era increased pressure for algorithmics to be taken seriously across an ever-expanding field of disciplines.[192] We have seen how the Constructionists were not satisfied with vague notions of the unity of art and science, as the artists of *Circle* had been, but instead preferred a more detailed engagement with specific specialties.[193] This sophistication proliferated across disciplines and sub-disciplines as researchers searched for and staked out areas of expertise.

New disciplines often begin with speculative leaps and exaggerated claims—in a word: polemics. At the outset of the structuralist craze, Lévi-Strauss's formula for "every myth" provoked strong reactions, but few anthropologists found it useful.[194] The imperative to research, however, renders provocative hypotheses difficult to ignore. After insinuating itself into the collective disciplinary consciousness, Lévi-Strauss's formula was recast as "the canonic formula for the structure of myth," and study of its viability became a sub-disciplinary cottage industry.[195] This dynamic played

---

191 For a history of this line of thinking, see Jameson, *Prison-House of Language*.

192 See, e.g., Arindam Dutta, "Linguistics, Not Grammatology: Architecture's A Prioris and Architecture's Priorities," in *A Second Modernism: MIT, Architecture, and the "Techno-Social" Moment*, ed. Arindam Dutta (Cambridge, MA: MIT Press, 2013), 1–70; Roger L. Geiger, *Research and Relevant Knowledge: American Research Universities since World War II* (Oxford: Oxford University Press, 1993).

193 Hill, the editor of *Data*, published academic papers on advanced topics in graph theory, for instance. See Frank Harary and Anthony Hill, "On the Number of Crossings in a Complete Graph," *Proceedings of the Edinburgh Mathematical Society* 13, no. 4 (December 1963): 333–38.

194 See Mark S. Mosko, "The Canonic Formula of Myth and Nonmyth," *American Ethnologist* 18, no. 1 (February 1991): 126–51. Looking back at the affair decades later, one observer noted that Lévi-Strauss's peers "wisely pretended the formula did not exist." Dan Sperber, *On Anthropological Knowledge* (Cambridge: Cambridge University Press, 1985), 65.

195 Mosko, "Canonic Formula of Myth," 126–27.

out across the university, and by the 1990s structuralist principles had been tested and absorbed in one form or another into the mainstream of most disciplines. This increasing sophistication of disciplinary knowledge led to greater (and perhaps unnecessary) precision in assumptions, methods, and results. When surveying the decades since the so-called quantitative turn swept the humanities and social sciences, it seems as if assumptions were systematically turned into axioms and methods into algorithms wherever possible.[196]

Supposing it was inevitable that architects would also turn to structuralist theory and specialized mathematical methods, some questions arise: What type of mathematics would it be? Would architects find uses for algorithmics? Certain long-standing preoccupations favored algorithmics—the previous chapters outline a few. Keeping in mind that genealogies necessarily branch erratically rather than converge on a single origin, we could add directions from two Bauhaus painting masters: Combining Kandinsky's fundamental elements of painting (the point, the line, and the plane; see fig. 28) with Klee's definition of a line ("taking a point for a walk"), we need only write instructions for *how points go on walks* to imagine an algorithmic approach to abstract art—and indeed this became one approach to computer art in the 1960s (fig. 29).[197]

So why did Klee, Kandinsky, and their students at the Bauhaus not produce algorithmic art in the 1920s? Britain in the 1960s added one crucial condition: The mood in architecture favored experimentation with bureaucratic organizational forms even within creative disciplines. Klee

---

196 For its impact on historiography, see Georg G. Iggers, *Historiography in the Twentieth Century: From Scientific Objectivity to the Postmodern Challenge* (Hanover: Wesleyan University Press, 1997).

197 Computation would be taught to architects in exactly this way in the 1980s. See William J. Mitchell, Robin S. Liggett, and Thomas Kvan, *The Art of Computer Graphics Programming: A Structured Introduction for Architects and Designers* (New York: Van Nostrand Reinhold, 1987). On the idea of genealogy, see Michel Foucault, "Nietzsche, Genealogy, History," in *The Essential Foucault* (New York: New Press, 1994), 351–69.

28 Oskar Schlemmer, *punkt – linie – fläche*, 1928, with a depiction of Wassily Kandinsky

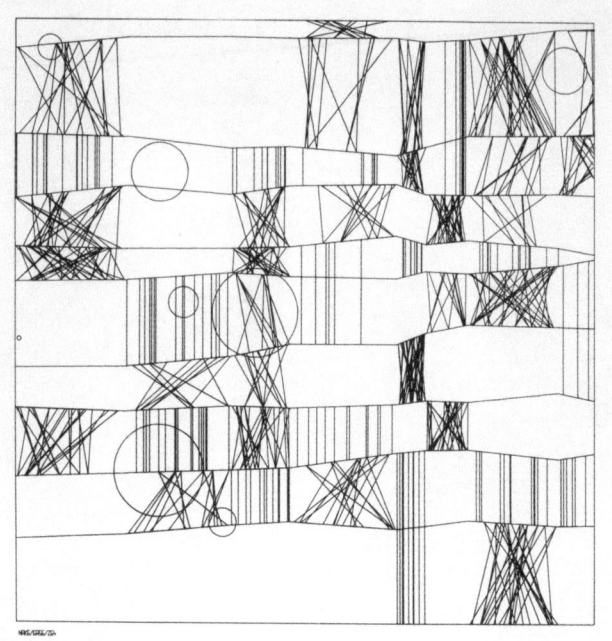

29 Frieder Nake, *Hommage à Paul Klee*, 13/9/65 Nr. 2, 1965

MOTIVATING THE ALGORITHM

30 Ernst Kállai, *Der Bauhausbuddha*, 1930, with Paul Klee depicted on the cloud

and Kandinsky were singular figures beholden to their artistic signatures, and they were in no hurry to formulate and share their artistic algorithms. Klee was notoriously obtuse: A caricature depicts him as "der Bauhausbuddha" floating in meditation above the school with students below praying for artistic inspiration (fig. 30).[198] Forty years later, such "poet innovators," as Summerson called them, were held in suspicion by a new generation of modernist artists and architects who sought instead to test the potentials of bureaucratic methods.

Another reason that algorithmic art was neglected until around 1960 is that, while drawings like Klee's sometimes appear systematic, there may have been little or no systematicity to their production. Motivation is crucial, but it is not enough. Working algorithmically means using algorithmic techniques, and the primary algorithmic techniques that found a place within architecture was the flowchart.

---

198 See Magdalena Droste, *Bauhaus, 1919–1933* (Cologne: Taschen, 1998), 62–65.

THE FLOWCHART
AS ALGORITHMIC
TECHNIQUE

The first flowcharts were developed in the field of scientific management, which began in the 1880s as an effort to rationalize workflows in manufacturing industries. The field's leading proponent, Frederick Winslow Taylor, was a management consultant who promised to boost labor productivity by "scientifically" studying the tasks that workers performed before providing "detailed instruction and supervision of each worker in the performance of that worker's discrete task."[199] The study of working processes took various forms. When the architectural historian Sigfried Giedion turned his attention to scientific management, he was especially enthralled by time-motion studies and their antecedents in photography, including the highly inventive work of Étienne-Jules Marey.[200] Many of these studies focused on the actions performed by a single worker, but sometimes it made sense to comprehensively map the entirety of a complex sequence involving numerous tasks. One exercise in this analytical effort would be to document the flow of materials through the process, paying special attention to inputs, outputs, and moments at which labor is applied along the way.

A method of comprehensively mapping such processes was introduced by the management consultants Frank and Lillian Gilbreth in a seminal 1921 paper on what they called "process charts." The Gilbreths used lines to represent movement from one step to the next and symbols to represent material inputs and actions that occur (fig. 31).[201] An accompanying chart explained the symbols—a dazzling variety of operations specific to the process in question (which, in their example, was the manufacture of rifle grenades). The

---

199 David Montgomery, *The Fall of the House of Labor: The Workplace, the State, and American Labor Activism, 1865–1925* (Cambridge: Cambridge University Press, 1987), 217.

200 Si[e]gfried Giedion, *Mechanization Takes Command: A Contribution to Anonymous History* (Oxford: Oxford University Press, 1948).

201 Frank B. Gilbreth and Lillian M. Gilbreth, *Process Charts* (New York: American Society of Mechanical Engineers, 1921), 12–13.

Gilbreths claimed that, with the right array of symbols, their flowcharts could encode routines of any type.

The Gilbreths' flowcharts were embedded within the larger apparatus of scientific management, and it was within this apparatus that managing flows became a legible "problem."[202] Consultants would study processes; managers and foremen would implement them; all sorts of paperwork would be required.[203] As careful accounting of material movement became standard managerial procedure, managers became acutely aware of bottlenecks. This occurred especially in the mid-nineteenth century in metalworking industries, where increasingly intense applications of heat meant that volumes of molten metal outpaced methods of using it. The resulting "crisis of control" in industrial production was avoided only in those industries "where the liquidity of flows facilitated their continued control even at vastly increased volumes and speeds."[204] It is often the case that a single step in a process determines the speed of the process as a whole, and scientific management tends to produce numerous "crisis" situations by speeding up one task at a time and thereby pressuring the other tasks to keep up.[205]

Although the Gilbreths' methods for working with processes found their way almost immediately into industrial engineering curricula and became standard techniques of management science already in the 1930s, their field of application was circumscribed.[206] Flowcharts are for the detailed

---

202 On the concept of "the apparatus," see Giorgio Agamben, *What Is an Apparatus?* (Redwood City: Stanford University Press, 2006).

203 The Gilbreths' 1921 paper includes examples of blank forms for ordering process changes, for instance.

204 Beniger, *Control Revolution*, 248.

205 The arrival of early computers often did this by increasing the speed of calculations that had previously been done manually, as in the famous story of "human computers" being replaced by the ENIAC (the Electronic Numerical Integrator and Computer completed in 1945) to eliminate a bottleneck in the computation of ballistic trajectories near the end of the Second World War. See Stan Augarten, *Bit by Bit: An Illustrated History of Computers* (New York: Ticknor & Fields, 1984), 210.

206 See Don B. Chaffin, "The Early Days of the Department of Industrial and Operations Engineering," in *The First 50 Years of the Department of Industrial and Operations Engineering at the University of Michigan: 1955–2005* (Ann Arbor:

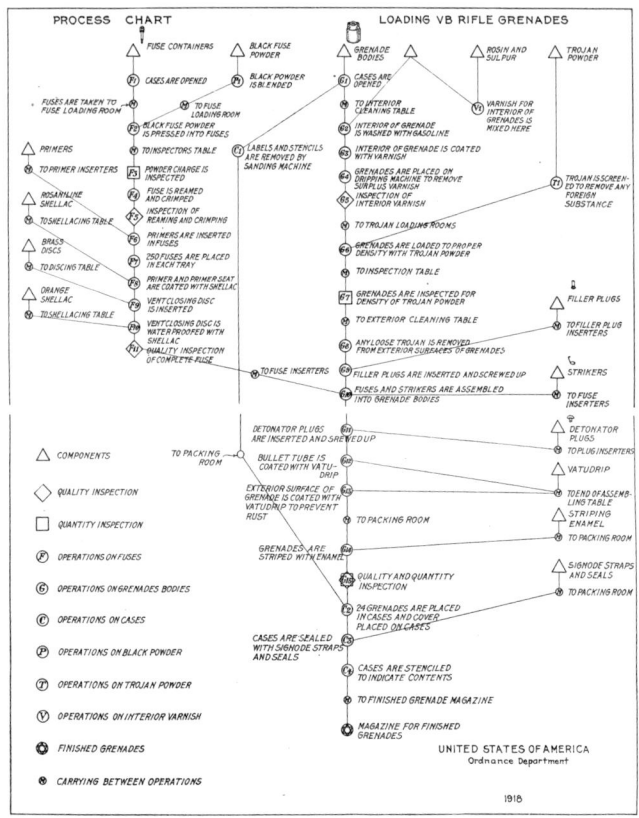

31 Frank Gilbreth and Lillian Gilbreth, process chart for loading rifle grenades, 1921

management of flows. It is worth distinguishing flowcharts from organization charts, which look similar but lack this crucial characteristic (unless it is something like authority that flows through the chart).

The organization chart was a mid-nineteenth-century invention modeled on genealogical and biological tree diagrams.[207] The earliest examples appeared following the growth of business enterprises and the increased specialization that resulted from new methods of technological control (like telegraphs and railway timetables) (fig. 32).[208] Organization charts made their way into architecture with the growth of corporate firms in the late nineteenth century, and exemplary models appeared in trade publications in the 1910s.[209] Thus the office of Albert Kahn published an organization chart in a 1938 issue of the *Architectural Forum* (fig. 33),[210] whereby Albert Kahn Associates embraced the ideology of organization more than most. Notice how the head of the firm—Albert Kahn, himself a registered architect—is given the title of Chief Administrator in the chart and identified in a photo caption as one among three administrators. Such self-

---

Michigan Publishing, 2015), http://dx.doi.org/10.3998/maize.13855463.0001.001. Early techniques for working with computational code took a unique form combining text and graphics. The first programmer, Ada Lovelace, wrote her programs for the first programmable computer, Charles Babbage's Difference Engine, using charts she invented for the purpose. See John Füegi and Jo Francis, "Lovelace & Babbage and the Creation of the 1843 'Notes'," *IEEE Annals of the History of Computing* 25, no. 4 (2003): 16–26.

207 The Scottish American engineer Daniel McCallum is credited with creating the first organization charts of American businesses around 1854. See Alfred D. Chandler, "Origins of the Organization Chart," *Harvard Business Review* 66, no. 2 (1988): 156–57; Ken Hopper and Will Hopper, "Dan McCallum Creates the Multidivisional Corporation," in *The Puritan Gift: Triumph, Collapse and Revival of an American Dream* (London: Tauris, 2007), 66–73.

208 Beniger, *Control Revolution*.

209 A model organization chart by Daniel Paul Higgins was published in the *Architectural Review* in 1916. See Michael Osman, *Modernism's Visible Hand: Architecture and Regulation in America* (Minneapolis: University of Minnesota Press, 2018), 174.

210 "Organization, Albert Kahn Inc.," *Architectural Forum* 69, no. 2 (August 1938): 91–96.

effacement was rare even among modernists who espoused doctrines of anonymous coordination.[211]

Encoded within the organization chart is a sociological theory which assumes that (1) society is systematically organized, (2) social systems can be divided analytically into discrete units, and (3) each unit serves a purpose or function within the social system as a whole. This is "structural functionalism," and it overlaps conceptually with functionalist theories of architecture.[212] Only a small step is required to imagine an organization chart as an architectural drawing: If we suppose that everyone in a firm has their own desk or office, the chart could neatly map onto a spatial diagram of workspaces and a functional diagram of lines of communication within the corporate hierarchy.[213] A similar line of reasoning would produce a chart mapping functional spaces in a house and circulation between them. Drawings in this manner were produced by the 1930s (fig. 34), and such organizational diagrams have been standard architecture school exercises since the 1960s.[214] Critiques of the ideology of functionalism and the impact of the aesthetics of organizations on architectural design gathered steam in

---

[211] Two others who thought and acted similarly were Walter Gropius at the Architects Collaborative and Leslie Martin at the London County Council. On the Architects Collaborative, see Michael Kubo, "The Anxiety of Anonymity: Bureaucracy and Genius in Late Modern Architecture Industry," in *New Constellations/New Ecologies, Proceedings of the 101st Annual Meeting of the ACSA* (Washington D.C.: ACSA, 2013), 810–17. On architecture and the London County Council, see Miles Glendinning, "Teamwork or Masterwork? The Design and Reception of the Royal Festival Hall," *Architectural History* 46 (2003): 277–319.

[212] On the term "function" in architecture, see Adrian Forty, *Words and Buildings: A Vocabulary of Modern Architecture* (London: Thames & Hudson, 2000), 174–95.

[213] For a study along these lines, see Osman, *Modernism's Visible Hand*, 165–84.

[214] See Paul Emmons, "The Cosmogony of Bubble Diagrams," in *Proceedings of the 86th ACSA Annual Meeting and Technology Conference* (Washington D.C.: ACSA, 1998), 420–25; Hyungmin Pai, *The Portfolio and the Diagram: Architecture, Discourse, and Modernity in America* (Cambridge, MA: MIT Press, 2002).

THE FLOWCHART AS ALGORITHMIC TECHNIQUE

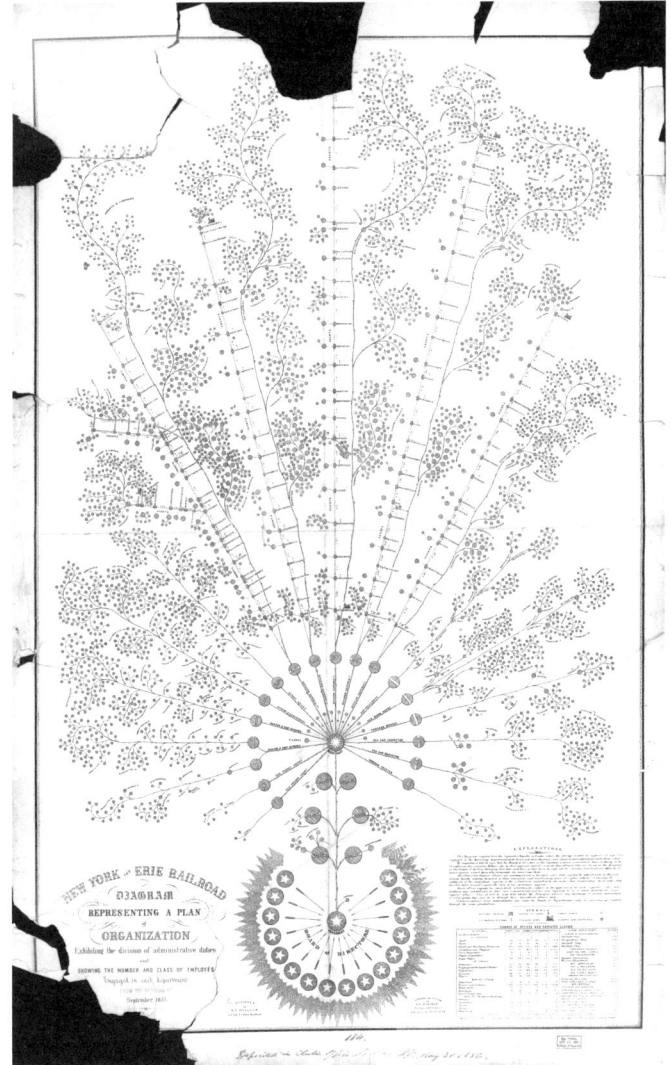

32 D. C. McCallum, New York and Erie Railroad diagram representing a plan of organization, 1855

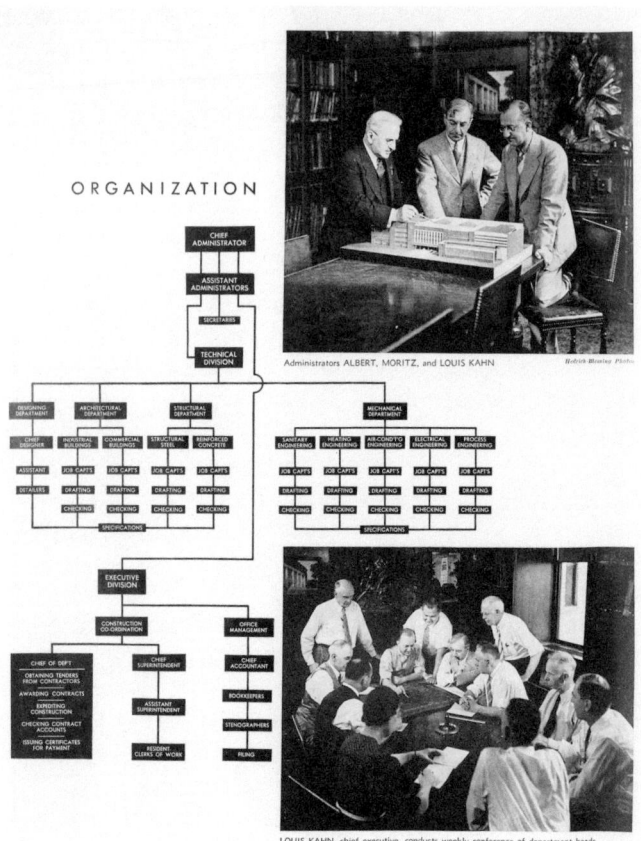

33 Albert Kahn Associates, organization chart, 1938

the 1960s and took center stage in the 1980s discourse on postmodernism.[215]

Architects have historically found fewer reasons to use flowcharts than organization charts. Rather than being generically spatial and functional, flowcharts deal with specific actions, inputs and outputs, and an accounting of material movement and transformation. There is no reason flowcharts cannot be spatialized, of course, and there are routing diagrams from the 1920s that map manufacturing processes within factory buildings in great detail (fig. 35).[216] Architectural design, however, typically begins by assuming a looser fit between spaces and activities.[217] This becomes clear when looking at Lillian Gilbreth's project to rationalize her kitchen, which she captured in a drawing of the "application of motion study to kitchen planning: making a cake" (fig. 36).[218] Her painstakingly detailed flowchart suggests only a minor re-arrangement of furniture, and the room itself is unchanged. And most activities are not nearly as rigidly prescribed as the steps for baking a cake.

So while organization charts have found a place in the architect's toolkit since the early decades of the twentieth century, flowcharts would enter into sustained use only much later.[219] Flipping through issues of the *Architectural Record* from the mid-1960s, organization charts appear in almost every issue but there is hardly a flowchart to be found. Occasionally diagrams show how projects "flow" through the corporate hierarchy of large firms, but these are best understood as flowchart icons: They are rhetorical devices—signifiers of the firm's organizational

---

215 See Klaus Herdeg, *The Decorated Diagram: Harvard Architecture and the Failure of the Bauhaus Legacy* (Cambridge, MA: MIT Press, 1983).
216 Pai discusses several examples in Pai, *Portfolio and Diagram*.
217 Pai, *Portfolio and Diagram*, 180.
218 Pai, *Portfolio and Diagram*, 182–84.
219 Flowcharts arguably only reached mainstream adoption with the use of Grasshopper (an add-on to McNeal's Rhinoceros 3D software) circa 2010.

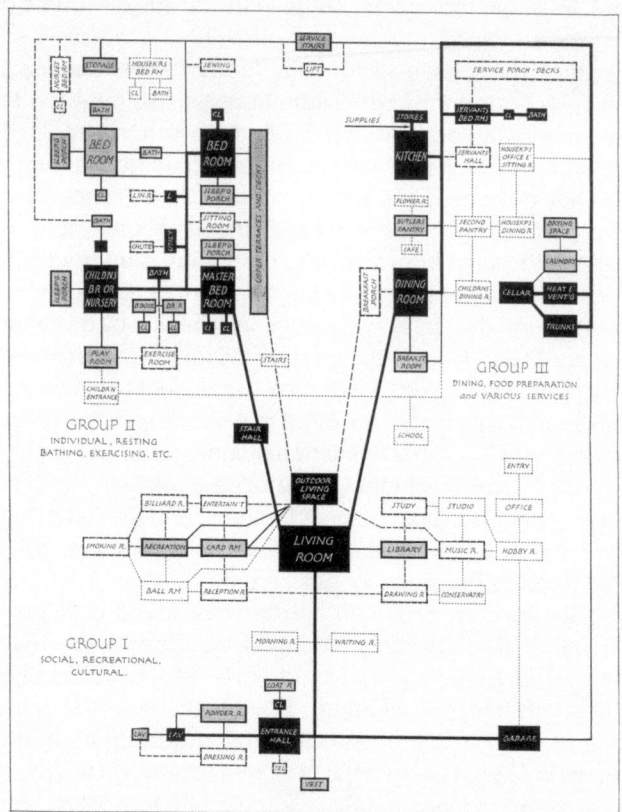

THE COUNTRY HOUSE CHART, ROOM BY ROOM

Functionally grouped, the various rooms of the country house, large or small, are shown diagrammatically in their relations with each other, for purposes of analysis and checking. The usual relative importance of the rooms is indicated by the relative blackness, the most essential rooms being solid black, next in importance, gray, etc.

34 Frederic Arden Pawley, "The Country House Chart, Room by Room," 1933

THE FLOWCHART AS ALGORITHMIC TECHNIQUE

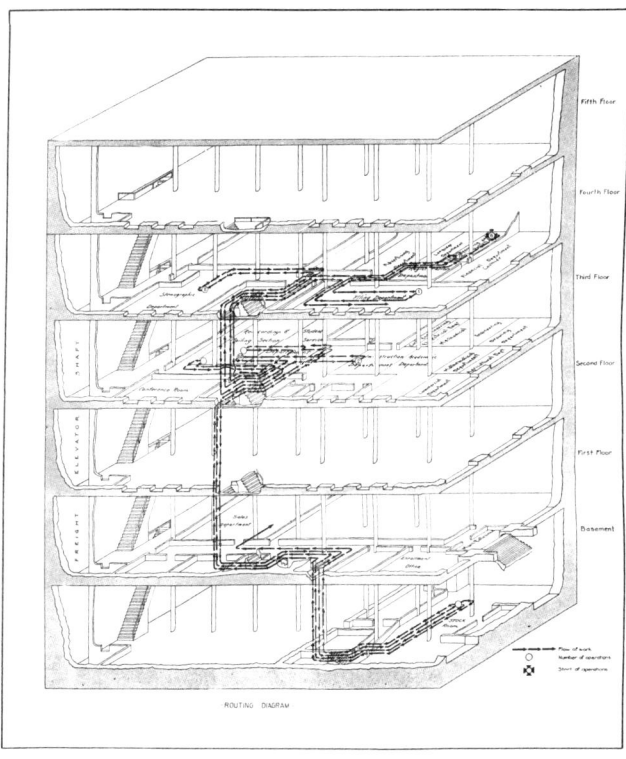

35 William Leffingwell, routing diagram, 1925

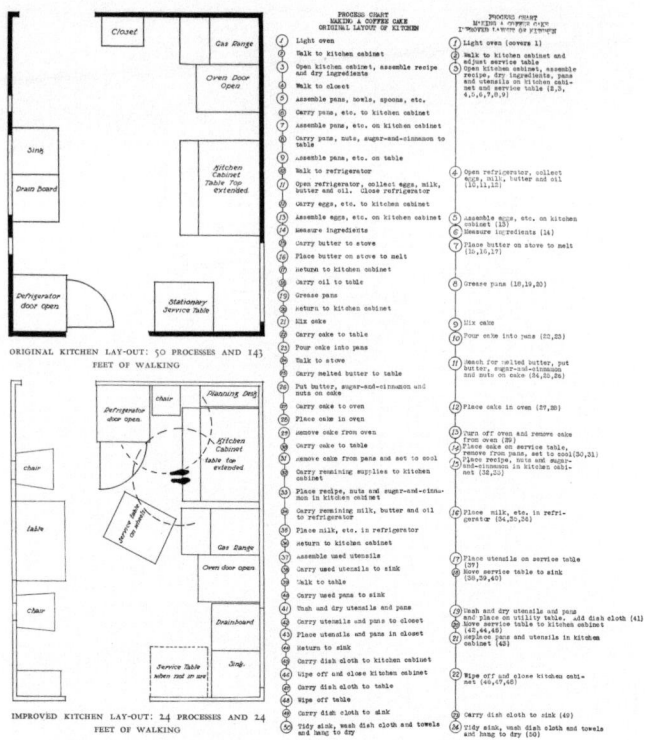

36 Lillian Gilbreth, application of motion study to kitchen planning: "Process Chart: Making a Coffee Cake," 1930

sophistication—and not useful instruments of corporate management or architectural design (fig. 37).

Flowcharts took on a new life with the advent of computation. Early computer programs remediated existing processes in digital form, as when "human computers" calculating ballistic trajectories were replaced by algorithms that could do the same.[220] As with scientific management a few decades earlier, the division of labor within elaborate corporate hierarchies was reflected in the nascent field of computer programming. Managers would have a general sense of what task needed to be performed, and they would leave the details of implementation to those more familiar with the processes themselves, whether they were engineers, mathematicians, or secretaries. John von Neumann, who famously specified the basic "architecture" of the modern electronic computer, used looping lines to represent recursivity in his computer programs, which were among the earliest, while leaving the practicalities to his subordinates (fig. 38).[221] (This created a loophole through which lower-level workers—often women and members of minority groups—became the first among the professional programmers that would be in high demand throughout the twentieth century.[222]) The field of computer programming was initially based on a feedback loop between high-level flowcharting and low-level coding, which came to be known as the "waterfall model" (fig.39). Neither the flowchart nor the computer program as it was implemented was a stand-alone entity, but—as with earlier scientific management—both were inextricable parts of a larger socio-technical apparatus.[223]

---

220 See David Alan Grier, *When Computers Were Human* (Princeton: Princeton University Press, 2010).
221 See Nathan Ensmenger, "The Multiple Meanings of a Flowchart," *Information & Culture: A Journal of History* 51, no. 3 (2016): 321–51.
222 See Jennifer S. Light, "When Computers Were Women," *Technology and Culture* 40, no. 3 (1999): 455–83.
223 For a primer on large socio-technical systems, see Paul N. Edwards, *A Vast Machine: Computer Models, Climate Data, and the Politics of Global Warming* (Cambridge, MA: MIT Press, 2010).

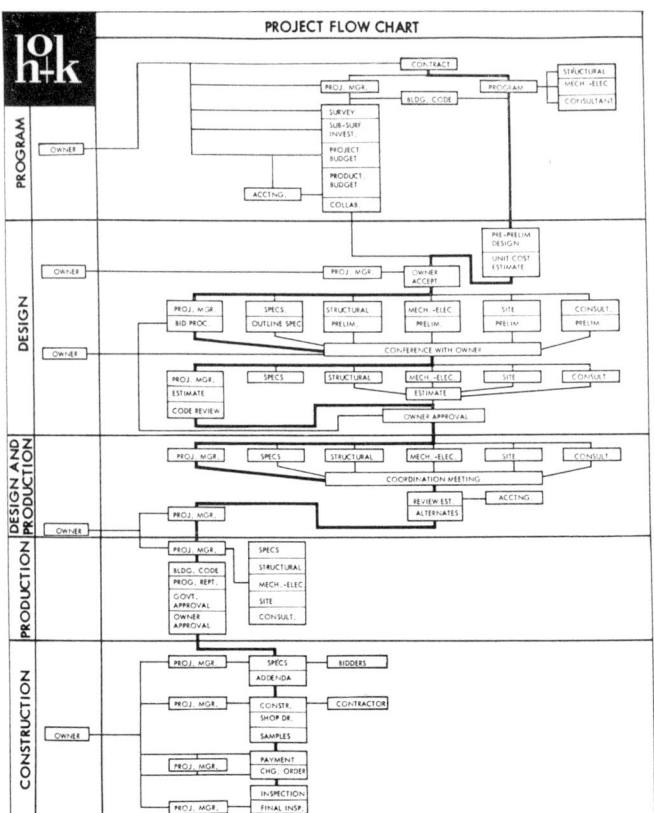

37 HOK, project flow chart, 1961

This is evident in the communication problems endemic to computer programming: The person who writes the codes needs to explain it to their teammates and their managers. The first successful commercial software package was a program to automatically translate code into flowcharts so the secretary who wrote it would not need to explain it to the boss herself (fig. 40).[224] Around 1970, flowcharts thus found a place as working documents in the middle of the software design and engineering process. (Software in this period referred not only to commercial software packages, but also to the programmers themselves, their knowledge, manuals, etc.—basically anything that was not hardware.[225]) Flowcharts were instrumental and ephemeral—more akin to an architectural working model or a sketch than the finished building (fig. 41).[226] Flowcharts depict the "idea" of a program while leaving out the details of implementation.

Flowcharts and codified programs go hand in hand: The former leave things vague (a lot of logic can be hidden inside a black box), while the latter—the code—is more closely associated with the mechanics or electronics of the assembly line or computing machine itself. As computer technology developed, several layers of abstraction were added between the plan of a program (the flowchart) and the electrical potentials represented by binary code. Low-level programming languages like assembly language provide only minimal abstraction from machine code; higher-level languages such as Fortran and C++ adhere more closely to the intuitive structure of spoken languages. Various practices of software architecture, software design, coding, programming, testing, and debugging fall in different places on the spectrum

---

224 The software was Autoflow, released by Applied Data Research (ADR) in 1965. Campbell-Kelly, *From Airline Reservations*, 57–58.

225 See Thomas Haigh, "Software in the 1960s as Concept, Service, and Product," *IEEE Annals of the History of Computing* 24, no. 1 (2002): 5–13.

226 A comparison could be made with screenshots: Matthew Allen, "Screenshot Aesthetic," in *MOS: Selected Works* (New York: Princeton Architectural Press, 2016), 271–76.

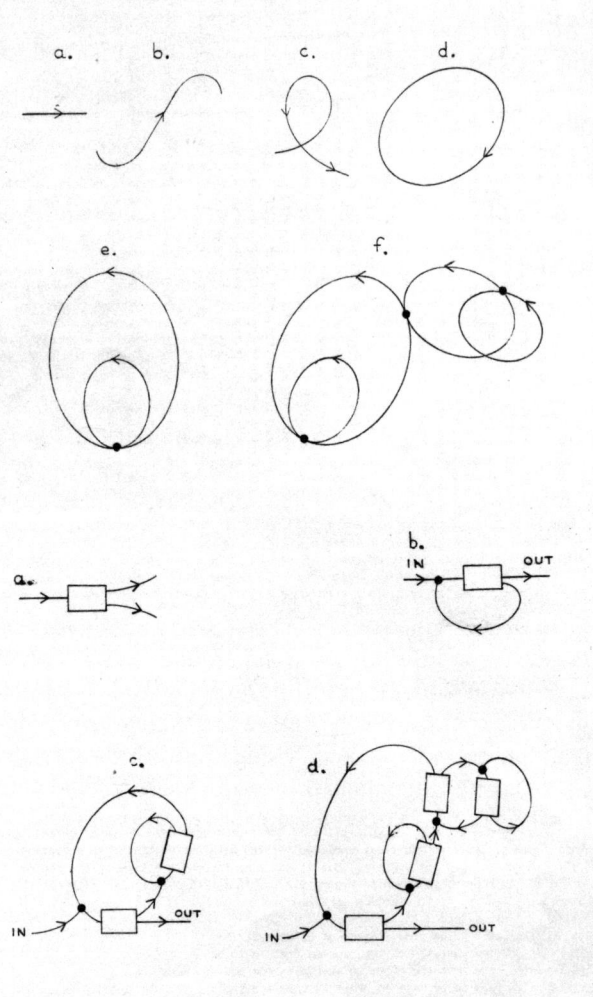

38 Herman H. Goldstine and John von Neumann, "Drawing Flow Diagrams," 1947

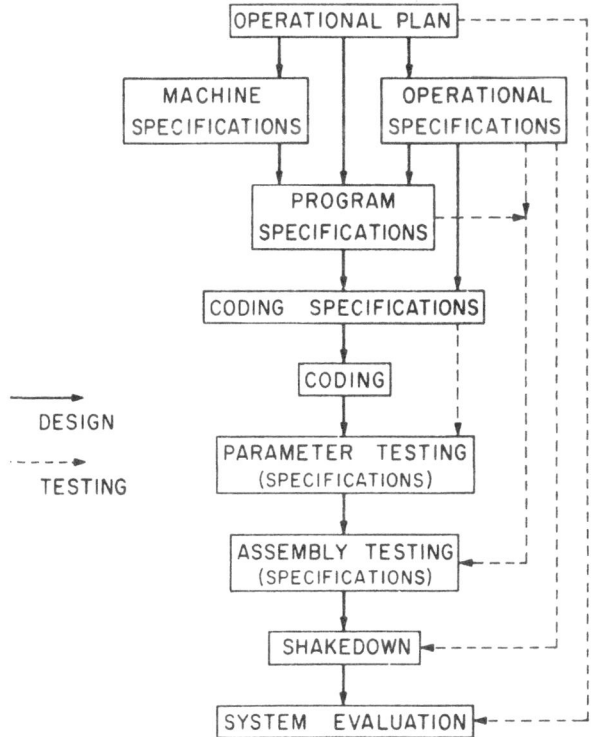

39 John F. Jacobs, "Program Production," 1981

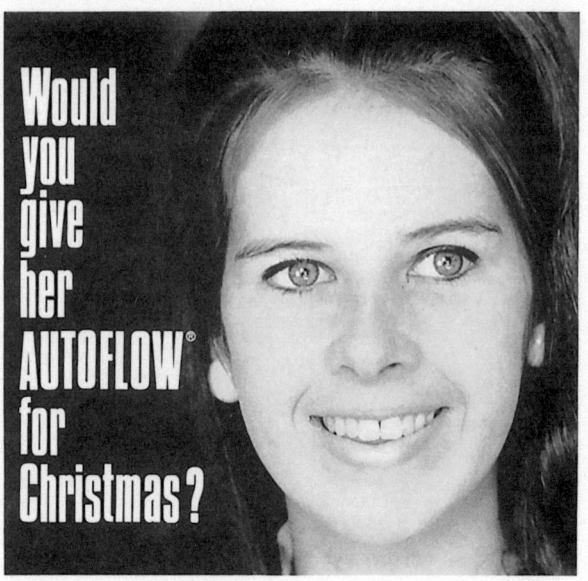

40 Applied Data Research, advertisement for Autoflow, c. 1975

THE FLOWCHART AS ALGORITHMIC TECHNIQUE

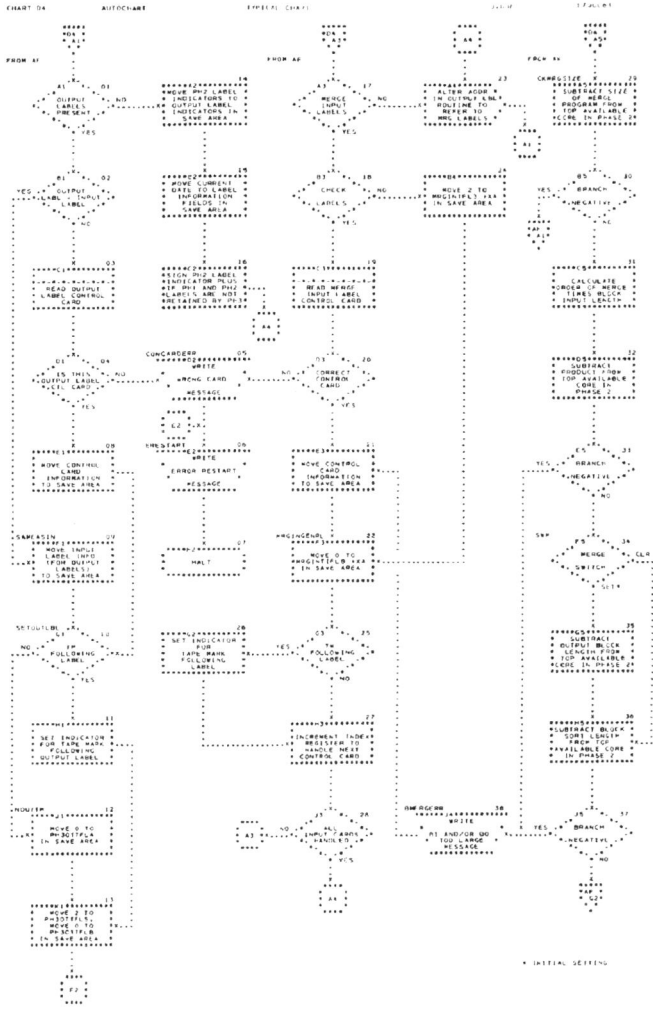

41 Christopher P. Smith, standard printer drawing, 1964

from the machinic to the human. It is in this middle zone of abstractions, and the middle levels of bureaucratic hierarchies, that we find the discipline of computer programming since the 1950s.[227] Commercial software packages quickly sprawled in complexity beyond any hope that either computer programs or the organizations that created them could be summarized in simple diagrams.

An important lesson from the history of computer programming is that, while algorithms do not strictly require computers (as they are simply lists of instructions), most advances in algorithmics have emerged from attempts to wrestle with practical problems encountered while programming actual computers. It is no coincidence that the concept of the algorithm was first formalized in mathematics alongside a description of a physical computing machine. Alan Turing's famous 1936 paper, "On Computable Numbers," hinges on a meta-problem of algorithmics: Is it possible to know before running a program whether a set of computational instructions will produce an answer rather than running fruitlessly in a loop forever?[228] Because this was a general question about all algorithms, Turing needed an equally general concept of a computational machine. His "universal Turing machine," as it is now called, consists of a "tape" (for storing symbols in memory), a device for reading from and writing to the tape (the "head"), a "table" of instructions, and a "state register" (for keeping track of which instruction is currently being executed). Once specified in this way as a concrete device, Turning was able to show that it is indeed not possible to know if an algorithm is computable or not. This was decisive: Turing proved that there is no substitute for running and testing an algorithm. Abstract mathematics

---

[227] See V.A. Uspenskii, "Algorithms, Theory of," in *Encyclopedia of Mathematics* (Berlin: Springer, 2002), http://encyclopediaofmath.org/index.php?title=Algorithms,_theory_of&oldid=45081.

[228] Alan Turing, "On Computable Numbers, with an Application to the Entscheidungsproblem," *Proceedings of the London Mathematical Society 42*, no. 1 (1937): 230–65.

cannot replace concrete programming.[229] As one path of research closed off, another path opened onto a set of practical questions: Can we find shortcuts to approximate answers in certain situations? Given specific computational hardware, generally how long will it take to run a given type of algorithm? If our program is taking too long to run, how can we make it more efficient? The discipline of algorithmics—a branch of computer science—had been established as a field of concrete experimentation to complement abstract mathematical speculation.

So while algorithms hold some interest at the most abstract level, there are many more discoveries to be made at each of the many levels of concreteness. In other words, most of the work in the discipline of algorithmics takes place in the same zone of abstraction as architecture. Looking back at Summerson's diagram of the flow of money in the building industry (see fig. 1), the architect's drawing set is pivotal, and the finished building is the goal, but most of the action takes place with the architect's staff and during the construction process. Architecture occurs between the sketch and the building just as algorithmics takes place between the initial flowchart and the final software program. As new computing hardware has been developed since the 1950s, there have been new potentials to be exploited with new tricks to be discovered, driving algorithmics forward as a discipline.

Another lesson from computer science is that what is construed as abstract at one level of analysis will be seen as concrete at another. An abstract flowchart can be translated into the concrete form of explicitly codified instructions; things that were only hinted at in the flowchart must be worked out more precisely in the process. The field of computer science is about managing translations between levels of abstraction, between possibilities and actualities. Algorithms are devices for translating between the abstract and

---

229 On this fascinating topic, see James H. Fetzer, "Program Verification: The Very Idea," *Communications of the ACM* 31, no. 9 (1988): 1048–63.

the concrete. Abstractly, computers can compute anything; writing an algorithm is a way of breaking a vague intention into a sequence of steps that can be concretely implemented. This top-down orientation is the bureaucratic aspect of algorithmics. The reverse is also true: "Anything" can be taken as raw material to be run through an algorithm. It is entirely in keeping with algorithmic thinking to work with the serial transformation of walls, columns, beams, and volumes (fig. 42). This is the bottom-up or "genius" aspect of algorithmics—its mechanism of charismatic revelation.[230]

In the period following the Second World War, the reach of algorithmics and the spread of general-purpose electronic computers largely coincided. In the 1950s, computer hardware matured along the lines described by von Neumann.[231] In the 1960s, the computer industry delivered thousands of (relatively) inexpensive and (relatively) easy to use computers to big businesses around the world. The decade opened with rare IBM mainframes filling entire rooms and programed with punch cards, and it closed with DEC minicomputers that fit under desks (barely), with keyboards, screens, mouses, printers, and fairly intuitive software. An ever more perfect medium for designing and implementing algorithms seemed to be spreading everywhere and evolving with no limit in sight.

Impressive hardware and sophisticated techniques would amount to nothing without the motivation to use them, however. Looking back at modernist art and architecture in the mid-twentieth century, formal proceduralism was rare in general, but it was a thriving practice within certain specific milieux. Concrete poetry was one apotheosis of procedural art. Moholy-Nagy's *Light Space Modulator* likewise provided a compelling conceptual model for the creation of sequences

---

[230] See Matthew Allen, "The Genius of Bureaucracy: SOM's Hajj Terminal and Geiger Berger Associates' Form-Finding Software," *Journal of the Society of Architectural Historians* 80, no. 4 (2021): 416–35.

[231] See Paul E. Ceruzzi, *A History of Modern Computing*, 2nd ed. (Cambridge, MA: MIT Press, 2003).

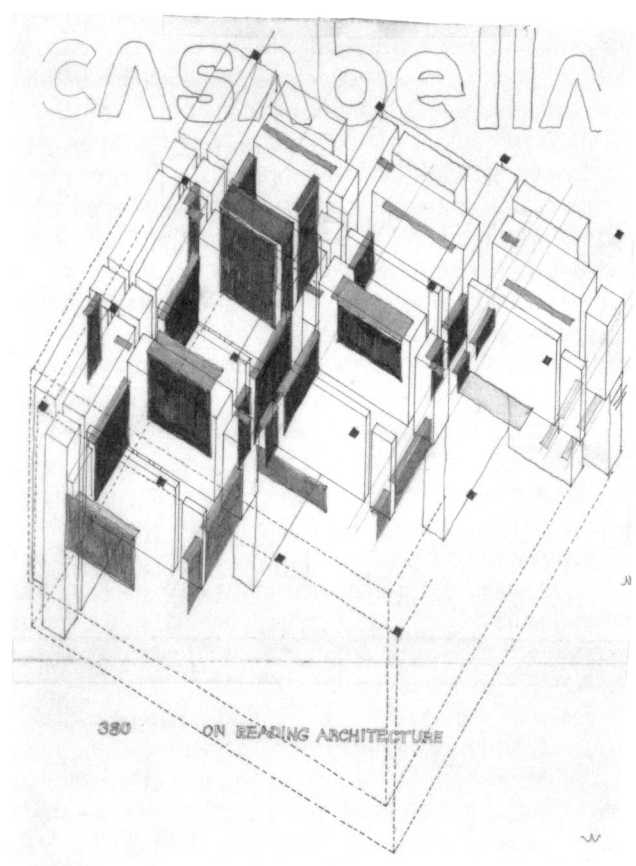

42 Peter Eisenman, axonometric for Falk House (House II) for *Casabella*, 1969–1970

of effects (fig. 5). A wide variety of artistic movements—experimentalism, conceptual art, performance art, systems aesthetics, computer art—developed similar ideas in different directions based on various artistic motivations.[232]

Here two meanings of the term "program" converge. First, following Mondrian, there are *artistic* programs: systematic attempts to move an artistic discipline toward a distant and difficult goal. Second, following Summerson, there are *architectural* programs: patterns of use specific to certain building types. The former is abstract, having to do with disciplinary objectives, while the latter deals more concretely with things in the world (people, spaces, buildings, cities). The two can be brought together: The Constructionists (artists like Hill and Molnar who dissected and reassembled Mondrian paintings) imagined that the discipline of art could make advances by specifying and testing the rules of specific visual or spatial types.

In architecture, another idea was often combined with this way of working: Progress was imagined to take place not only within the discipline of architecture but also within society at large. Focusing on organization and making progress in building typology and the organization of architectural bureaucracies would result, as Summerson argued, in a better built environment for everyone.[233] It was this combined programmatic approach—bringing together an internal, disciplinary program of formal, typological development with an external program of social progress—that animated the first era of algorithmic architecture.

---

232 See, e.g., Jack Burnham, *Software: Information Technology; Its New Meaning for Art* (New York: Jewish Museum, 1970).
233 Summerson, "Bread & Butter."

PROGRAMMING
ARCHITECTURE

When were algorithms first used to design architecture? This is not a particularly useful question insofar as any step-by-step recipe for architecture would count as an algorithm; it would be no surprise to find such a recipe in even the unlikeliest times and places. But in narrowing the focus to this story's principal setting in 1960s Cambridge, two projects jump out as novelties. The first is a scheme for generating new buildings in the idiom of Frank Lloyd Wright, which was published in a mathematics textbook for architects written by Philip Steadman (editor of *Form*) and his colleague at the University of Cambridge, the architect Lionel March.[234] It begins with an analysis of four geometrically related floorplans by Wright (fig. 43). March and Steadman describe Wright's algorithms in a mix of words and math:

> Wright spins the original quadruple unit though a half-turn, but this time the centre of rotation is even more eccentric and the resulting unit is more elongated than in the Chicago apartment. The plan now contains twelve hotel suites. The fire-escapes are external and one of the structural shafts is removed from each quadruple, thus making room for a central corridor. The symmetry of the unit is again C2. This unit is essentially translated in two directions, T1 and T2. The development is T1–2, T1–1, I = T10, T11, T12 and T13 and I = T20, T21, T22, T23.[235]

Although it requires careful attention to decode, their account is an exceptionally clear formulation of an algorithm for architectural design—the sequence of steps Wright enacted to arrive at the plan for his Crystal Heights hotel and housing project. Through their analysis, Steadman and March build a conceptual bridge between modernism, with its mostly

---

234 On Lionel March, who worked in the office of Leslie Martin, see Sharr, *Demolishing Whitehall*.

235 Lionel March and Philip Steadman, *The Geometry of Environment: An Introduction to Spatial Organization in Design* (London: RIBA, 1971), 85.

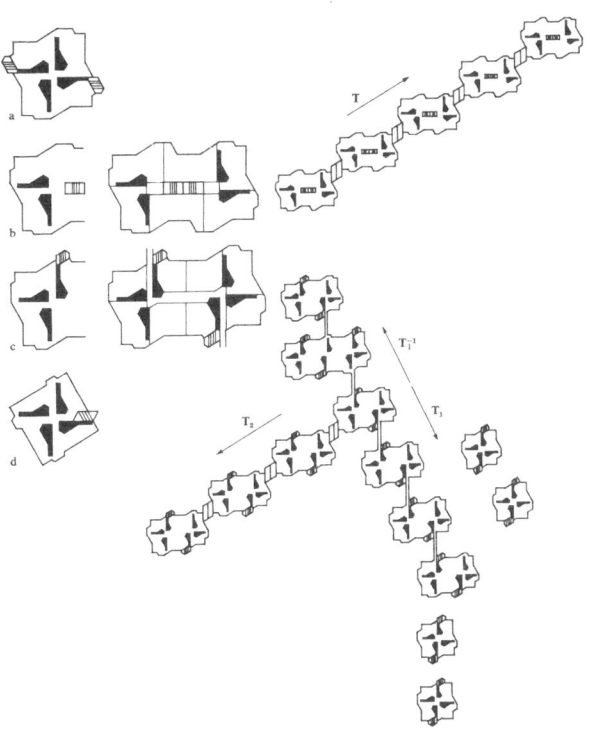

43 Lionel March and Philip Steadman, "The Generic Plans of Buildings and Projects by Frank Lloyd Wright," 1971

implicit codes and rules, and what would later be called parametricism, in which algorithmic thinking takes center stage. They summarize: "The two greatest form-makers of twentieth-century architecture—Frank Lloyd Wright and Le Corbusier—were able to innovate largely because of their appreciation and deep understanding of symmetry and pattern-structure."[236] By explicating the "pattern-structure" of Wright's plans, new Wrightian buildings could be produced by simply tweaking the code. This has been the thesis of this essay: an algorithmic approach to design developed within architecture as a means of taking the next step in the modernist progressive agenda by understanding the programmatic code at the heart of geometrical form.

A second remarkable project expanded the scope of this endeavor beyond canonically "great" buildings: an algorithm for designing a university. The algorithm takes the form of a book, and it begins with a graphical index styled as a flowchart that depicts the flow of the design (fig. 44).[237] The architect works from left to right, with one aspect of the design problem leading to the next along the flowchart's lines: Analyze the context (the university's location in the city, who the students are, etc.), study the day-to-day activities of the school (going to class, eating, sleeping, etc.), design the "building geometry," evaluate the results, and if necessary loop back to address deficiencies. The algorithm here is the entire design process, which aims not just for a collection of buildings but for a thriving academic community. Steadman and his coauthors present a methodological answer to the conundrum Summerson had identified a decade earlier: How, in practical terms, can architects turn away from geometrical form and towards "rhythmically repetitive patterns?"[238] How can architects design "the whole

---

236 March and Steadman, *Geometry of Environment*, 85.

237 Nicholas Bullock, Peter Dickens, and Philip Steadman, *A Theoretical Basis for University Planning* (Cambridge: Cambridge University School of Architecture, 1968).

238 Summerson, "Case for a Theory," 309.

PROGRAMMING ARCHITECTURE

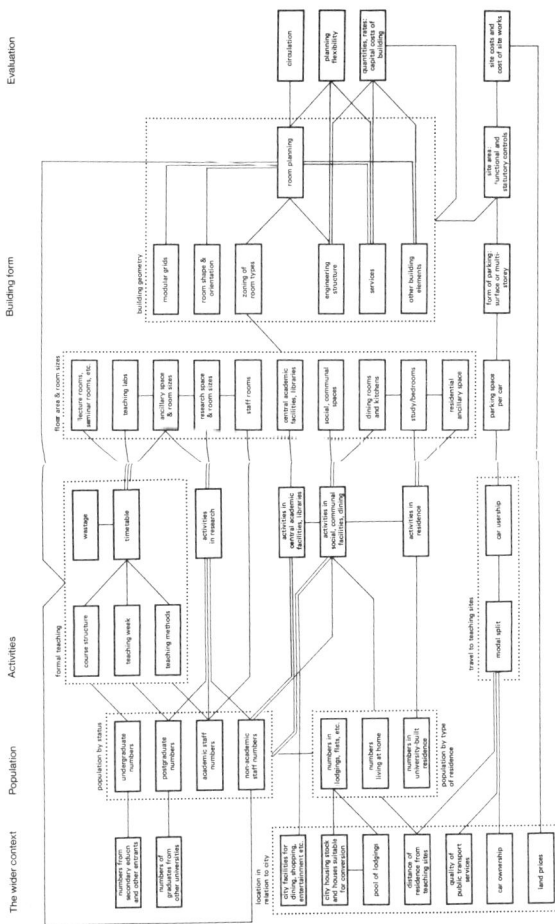

44 Nicholas Bullock, Peter Dickens, and Philip Steadman, graphical index for *A Theoretical Basis for University Planning*, 1968

material environment" and "every building activity in the country?" How, in short, can the program become "the architect's medium?"[239] *A Theoretical Basis for University Planning* aimed to show architects how. The answer was to redesign the algorithm of architectural design.

Flowcharts nudged architects to think beyond artificial limits to the scope of design. Once inputs and outputs begin to be considered, the systems within which buildings are located are seen to extend far beyond the physical footprint. The ultimate scope of algorithmic design is best illustrated by one of the most iconic flowcharts of all time: the DYNAMO flow diagram of the World3 model (fig. 45), which accompanied *Dynamics of Growth in a Finite World*, the third volume in the book series that began with the bestselling *Limits to Growth*.[240] Released a decade after Rachel Carson's *Silent Spring*, it brought systematic clarity to a field with no lack of personal, visceral, emotional resonance. The flowchart depicts a simulation system written in the programming language DYNAMO that modeled future levels of pollution, resource stocks, and more over a span of several decades, building on then-current trends. It famously predicted collapse. The simulation had its problems (for instance, the greenhouse effect was not on the authors' radar), but the thrust of the research, as summarized in the book's brief conclusion, is as lucid today as fifty years ago:

> Systems understanding must be coupled with still another effort, the greatest of all—the construction of a consistent, feasible set of long term values for human society. Under the false assumption that everything can be maximized for everyone with sufficient material growth, the present, temporary period of

[239] Summerson, "Introduction," 11.
[240] Dennis Meadows et al., *Dynamics of Growth in a Finite World* (Cambridge, MA: Wright-Allen, 1974); Donella Meadows et al., *The Limits to Growth: A Report for the Club of Rome's Project on the Predicament of Mankind* (New York: Universe Books, 1972).

PROGRAMMING ARCHITECTURE

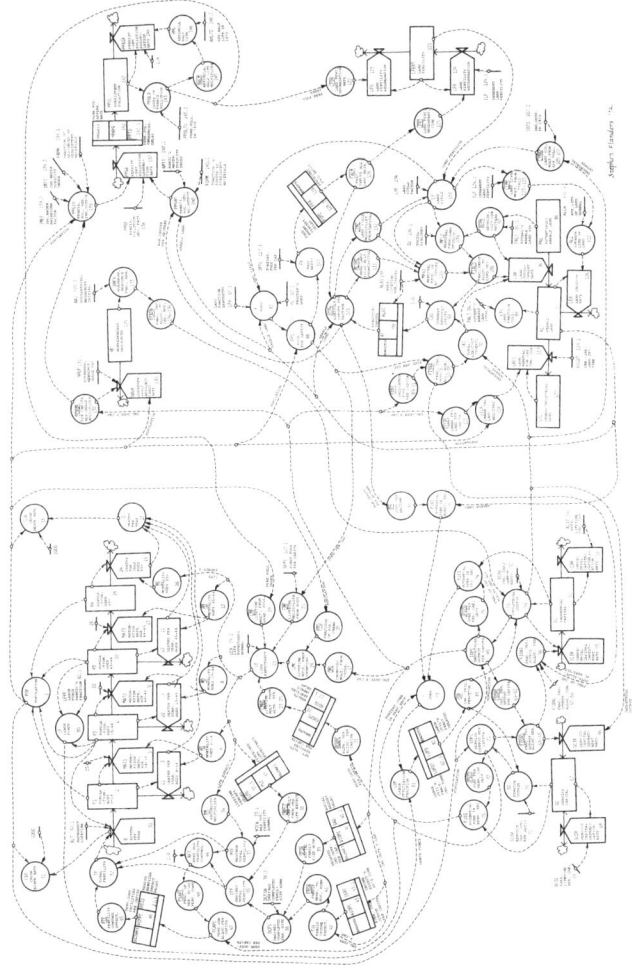

45 Stephen Flanders, DYNAMO flow diagram of the World3 model, 1972

material growth has allowed social institutions to avoid all discussion of ultimate goals and value conflicts. The transition to equilibrium must begin with a broad discussion of what is and is not important to human society, where priorities lie, how trade-offs are to be made, and in what condition the human race would like to find itself when growth on this finite earth finally ceases.[241]

Around 1970, applying calculated logic to such an emotionally charged topic came as a shock. How can human values or nature itself be so coldly quantified? This shock accompanied early algorithmic art and architecture as well: How can artistic merit be calculated? The problem is now quite the opposite: The discipline of architecture has developed effective means by which to sideline algorithmic design, casting it either as a dryly technical branch of building science or as an "interesting" but limited technique for generating surprising sketches.[242] Either way, it poses no real challenge to mainstream architecture.

—

Recovering the history of flowcharting shows that algorithmics is not a mere curiosity but rather an essential element of how artists and architects have grappled with modernity. Many of the ideas that motivated abstract art were shared with modern architecture and led directly to algorithmic design—it was the next logical step. They continued to evolve through postmodernism and deconstruction and into the digital 1990s. The notion that architecture is about organization rather than image remains as potent as ever.

The tragedy here has not to do with disciplinary politics but with how the world around us is shaped and by whom.

241 Dennis Meadows et al., *Dynamics of Growth*, 564.
242 On "the interesting," see Sianne Ngai, "Merely Interesting," *Critical Inquiry* 34, no. 4 (2008): 777–817.

Mainstream consensus dismissed modernism as hubristic social engineering, but increasingly untenable environments——embedded within global systems of all sorts—continue to be constructed without architects' involvement. The reigning fantasy has been that leaving everything to "the market" is the best idea, with the predictable result that the most consequential decisions with respect to global systems are made by billionaires and the corporations they control. Meanwhile, systemic problems—the climate crisis, ecosystem collapse, social injustice, and the adverse effects of global computation—continue to deepen. Architects already play a role in the design of the systems that shape our environments, and perhaps their role should be larger—but only if it is also more thoughtful. Flowcharting, the technique for working with the flows that animate the world, provides conceptual tools commensurate with the task.

ANNEX

BIBLIOGRAPHY

Agamben, Giorgio. *What Is an Apparatus?* Redwood City: Stanford University Press, 2006.

Agar, Jon. "What Difference Did Computers Make?" *Social Studies of Science* 36, no. 6 (December 2006): 869–907.

Alexander, Christopher. "A Much Asked Question about Computers and Design." In *Architecture and the Computer: Proceedings of the First Boston Architectural Center Conference*, 52–54. Boston: Boston Architectural Center, 1964.

Allen, Matthew. "Representing Computer-Aided Design: Screenshots and the Interactive Computer circa 1960." *Perspectives on Science* 24, no. 6 (2016): 637–68.

Allen, Matthew. "Screenshot Aesthetic." In *MOS: Selected Works*, 271–76. New York: Princeton Architectural Press, 2016.

Allen, Matthew. "The Genius of Bureaucracy: SOM's Hajj Terminal and Geiger Berger Associates' Form-Finding Software." *Journal of the Society of Architectural Historians* 80, no. 4 (2021): 416–35.

Angius, Nicola, Giuseppe Primiero, and Raymond Turner. "The Philosophy of Computer Science." In *The Stanford Encyclopedia of Philosophy*, edited by Edward N. Zalta: Metaphysics Research Lab, Stanford University, 2021. https://plato.stanford.edu/archives/spr2021/entries/computer-science/.

Architectural Forum. "Organization, Albert Kahn Inc." 69, no. 2 (August 1938): 91–96.

Arp, Jean. "Abstract Art, Concrete Art." In *Art of This Century: Objects, Drawings, Photographs, Paintings, Sculptures, Collages, 1910 to 1942*, edited by Peggy Guggenheim, 29–31. New York: Art of This Century, 1942.

Augarten, Stan. *Bit by Bit: An Illustrated History of Computers*. New York: Ticknor & Fields, 1984.

Bann, Stephen. "Communication and Structure in Concrete Poetry." *Image*, Special issue, *Kinetic Art: Concrete Poetry* 1964, 8–9.

Barr, Alfred H. *Cubism and Abstract Art; Painting, Sculpture, Constructions, Photography, Architecture, Industrial Art, Theatre, Films, Posters, Typography*. New York: Museum of Modern Art, 1936.

Barthes, Roland. "The Activity of Structuralism." Translated by Stephen Bann. *Form* 1 (1966): 12–13.

Beniger, James R. *The Control Revolution: Technological and Economic Origins of the Information Society*. Cambridge, MA: Harvard University Press, 1986.

Bois, Yve-Alain. "Mondrian and the Theory of Architecture." *Assemblage* 4 (October 1987): 102–30.

Bois, Yve-Alain. "Russian Revolution: On the Politics of Constructivism." *Artforum* 44, no. 6 (February 2006): 53–58.

Broeckmann, Andreas. *Machine Art in the Twentieth Century*. Cambridge, MA: MIT Press, 2016.

Brouwer, L. E. J. "Consciousness, Philosophy and Mathematics." In *Data: Directions in Art, Theory and Aesthetics*, edited by Anthony Hill, 12–21. London: Faber & Faber, 1968.

Brüning, Ute. "Herbert Bayer." In *Bauhaus*, edited by Jeannine Fiedler and Peter Feierabend, 332–41. Cologne: Könemann, 2000.

Buchloh, Benjamin H.D. "Cold War Constructivism." In *Reconstructing Modernism: Art in New York, Paris, and Montreal, 1945–1964*, edited by Serge Guilbaut, 85–112. Cambridge, MA: MIT Press, 1990.

Bullock, Nicholas, Peter Dickens, and Philip Steadman. *A Theoretical Basis for University Planning*. Cambridge: Cambridge University School of Architecture, 1968.

Bürger, Peter. *Theorie der Avantgarde*. Frankfurt: Suhrkamp, 1974.

Burnham, Jack. *Software: Information Technology; Its New Meaning for Art*. New York: Jewish Museum, 1970.

Campbell-Kelly, Martin. *From Airline Reservations to Sonic the Hedgehog: A History of the Software Industry*. Cambridge, MA: MIT Press, 2003.

Cardoso Llach, Daniel. *Builders of the Vision: Software and the Imagination of Design*. London: Routledge, 2015.

Carolin, Peter. "Martin, Sir (John) Leslie." In *Oxford Dictionary of National Biography*. Oxford: Oxford University Press, 2013. https://doi.org/10.1093/ref:odnb/74528.

Ceruzzi, Paul E. *A History of Modern Computing*. 2nd ed. Cambridge, MA: MIT Press, 2003.

Chabert, Jean-Luc, ed. *A History of Algorithms: From the Pebble to the Microchip*. Berlin: Springer, 1999.

Chaffin, Don B. "The Early Days of the Department of Industrial and Operations Engineering." In *The First 50 Years of the Department of Industrial and Operations Engineering at the University of Michigan: 1955–2005*. Ann Arbor: Michigan Publishing, 2015. http://dx.doi.org/10.3998/maize.13855463.0001.001.

Chandler, Alfred D. "Origins of the Organization Chart." *Harvard Business Review* 66, no. 2 (1988): 156–57.

Cobbing, Bob. *Changing Forms in English Visual Poetry: The Influence of Tools and Machines*. London: Writers Forum, 1988.

Colomina, Beatriz. *Clip, Stamp, Fold: The Radical Architecture of Little Magazines, 196X to 197X*. Barcelona: Actar, 2011.

Corry, Leo. *Modern Algebra and the Rise of Mathematical Structures*. 2nd ed. Basel: Birkhäuser, 2004.

Cumming, Carolyn. "Experimental Aesthetics." *Form* 1 (1966): 14–15.

Debord, Guy. "Constant and the Path of Unitary Urbanism." Translated by Brian Holms. *NOT BORED!* 28 (1997). http://www.notbored.org/constant-debord.html.

Deleuze, Gilles. "How Do We Recognize Structuralism?" Translated by Michael Taormina. In *Desert Islands, and Other Texts (1953–1974)*, edited by David Lapoujade, 170–92. Los Angeles: Semiotext(e), 2004.

Difford, Richard. "Developed Space: Theo van Doesburg and the Chambre de Fleurs." *The Journal of Architecture* 12, no. 1 (2007): 79–98.

Doesburg, Theo van. "Film as Pure Form." *Form* 1 (1966): 5–11.

Dosse, Francois. *History of Structuralism, vol 1: The Rising Sign, 1945–1966*. Minneapolis: University of Minnesota Press, 1997.

Draper, R. P. "Concrete Poetry." *New Literary History* 2, no. 2 (1971): 329–40.

Droste, Magdalena. *Bauhaus, 1919–1933*. Cologne: Taschen, 1998.

Dupré, John. *Human Nature and the Limits of Science*. Oxford: Clarendon, 2001.

Dutta, Arindam. "Linguistics, Not Grammatology: Architecture's A Prioris and Architecture's Priorities." In *A Second Modernism: MIT, Architecture, and the "Techno-Social" Moment*, edited by Arindam Dutta, 1–70. Cambridge, MA: MIT Press, 2013.

Edwards, Paul N. *A Vast Machine: Computer Models, Climate Data, and the Politics of Global Warming*. Cambridge, MA: MIT Press, 2010.

Edwards, Paul N. *The Closed World: Computers and the Politics of Discourse in Cold War America*. Cambridge, MA: MIT Press, 1996.

Ellis, R. J. "Mapping the United Kingdom Little Magazine Field." In *New British Poetries: The Scope of the Possible*, edited by Robert Hampson and Peter Barry, 72–102. Manchester: University of Manchester Press, 1993.

Emmons, Paul. "The Cosmogony of Bubble Diagrams." In *Proceedings of the 86th ACSA Annual Meeting and Technology Conference*, 420–25. Washington D.C. ACSA, 1998.

Ensmenger, Nathan. "The Multiple Meanings of a Flowchart." *Information & Culture: A Journal of History* 51, no. 3 (2016): 321–51.

Ernest, John. "Some Thoughts on Mathematics." *Structure* 3, no. 2 (1961): 49–51.

Exhibition of Works by the Italian Futurist Painters. London: Sackville Gallery, 1912.

Fetzer, James H. "Program Verification: The Very Idea." *Communications of the ACM* 31, no. 9 (1988): 1048–63.

Forty, Adrian. *Words and Buildings: A Vocabulary of Modern Architecture*. London: Thames & Hudson, 2000.

Foster, Hal, Rosalind Krauss, Yve-Alain Bois, Benjamin H.D. Buchloh, and David Joselit. *Art since 1900: Modernism, Antimodernism, Postmodernism*. London: Thames & Hudson, 2004.

Foucault, Michel. "Nietzsche, Genealogy, History." In *The Essential Foucault*, 351–69. New York: New Press, 1994.

Foucault, Michel. *The Order of Things: An Archaeology of Human Sciences*. Translated by Alan Sheridan. New York: Pantheon, 1970.

Fowler, Alan, ed. *A Rational Aesthetic: The Systems Group and Associated Artists*. Southampton: Southampton City Art Gallery, 2008.

Füegi, John, and Jo Francis. "Lovelace & Babbage and the Creation of the 1843 'Notes.'" *IEEE Annals of the History of Computing* 25, no. 4 (2003): 16–26.

Galison, Peter. *Image and Logic: A Material Culture of Microphysics*. Chicago: University of Chicago Press, 1997.

Geertz, Clifford. "Deep Play: Notes on the Balinese Cockfight." *Daedalus* 101, no. 1 (1972): 1–37.

Geiger, Roger L. *Research and Relevant Knowledge: American Research Universities since World War II*. Oxford: Oxford University Press, 1993.

Giedion, Si[e]gfried. *Mechanization Takes Command: A Contribution to Anonymous History*. Oxford: Oxford University Press, 1948.

Giedion, Si[e]gfried. "The Work of the C.I.A.M." In *Circle: International Survey of Constructive Art*, edited by Leslie Martin, Ben Nicholson, and Naum Gabo, 272–78. London: Faber & Faber, 1937.

Gilbert, Basil. "The Reflected Light Compositions of Ludwig Hirschfeld-Mack." *Form* 2 (1966): 10–13.

Gilbreth, Frank B., and Lillian M. Gilbreth. *Process Charts*. New York: American Society of Mechanical Engineers, 1921.

Glendinning, Miles. "Teamwork or Masterwork? The Design and Reception of the Royal Festival Hall." *Architectural History* 46 (2003): 277–319.

Gombrich, E.H., and Ruth Shaw. "Symposium: Art and the Language of the Emotions." In *Proceedings of the Aristotelian Society, Supplementary*, 215–46. Vol. 36. 1962.

Grandal Montero, Gustavo. "From Cambridge to Brighton: Concrete Poetry in Britain, an Interview with Stephen Bann." In *Artist's Book Yearbook 2016–2017*, 70–93. Bristol: Impact Press, 2015.

Gray, Crispin. "Computers and Design." *Form* 1 (1966): 19–22.

Green, Christopher, and Barnaby Wright, eds. *Mondrian/Nicholson: In Parallel*. London: Courtauld Gallery, 2012.

Greenberg, Clement. "Modernist Painting." *Arts Yearbook* 4 (1961): 101–8.

Grier, David Alan. *When Computers Were Human*. Princeton: Princeton University Press, 2010.

Grieve, Alastaire. *Constructed Abstract Art in England After the Second World War: A Neglected Avant-Garde*. New Haven: Yale University Press, 2005.

Gropius, Walter. "Art Education and State." In *Circle: International Survey of Constructive Art*, edited by Leslie Martin, Ben Nicholson, and Naum Gabo, 238–42. London: Faber & Faber, 1937.

Gropius, Walter. "Programme of the Staatliches Bauhaus in Weimar." In *Programs and Manifestoes on 20th-Century Architecture*, edited by Ulrich Conrads, 49–53. Cambridge, MA: MIT Press, 1971.

Guillory, John. "Genesis of the Media Concept." *Critical Inquiry* 36 (2010): 321–62.

Haigh, Thomas. "Software in the 1960s as Concept, Service, and Product." *IEEE Annals of the History of Computing* 24, no. 1 (2002): 5–13.

Hall, Stuart, ed. *Representation: Cultural Representations and Signifying Practices*. London: Sage, 1997.

Hanna, Robert. "Kant's Theory of Judgment." In *Stanford Encyclopedia of Philosophy*. 2017. https://plato.stanford.edu/archives/win2017/entries/kant-judgment/.

Harary, Frank, and Anthony Hill. "On the Number of Crossings in a Complete Graph." *Proceedings of the Edinburgh Mathematical Society* 13, no. 4 (December 1963): 333–38.

Harwood, Elain. "London County Council Architects." In *Oxford Dictionary of National Biography*. Oxford: Oxford University Press, 2009. https://doi.org/10.1093/ref:odnb/97268.

Harwood, John. *The Interface: IBM and the Transformation of Corporate Design, 1945–1976*. Minneapolis: University of Minnesota Press, 2016.

Heller, Steven. *Merz to Emigre and Beyond: Avant-Garde Magazine Design of the Twentieth Century*. London: Phaidon, 2003.

Herdeg, Klaus. *The Decorated Diagram: Harvard Architecture and the Failure of the Bauhaus Legacy*. Cambridge, MA: MIT Press, 1983.

Hesse, Mary B. *Models and Analogies in Science*. London: Sheed & Ward, 1963.

Hilder, Jamie. *Designed Words for a Designed World: The International Concrete Poetry Movement, 1955–1971*. Montreal: McGill-Queen's University Press, 2016.

Hill, Anthony. "Art and Mathesis: Mondrian's Structures." *Leonardo* 1, no. 3 (July 1968): 233–42.

Hill, Anthony. "Constructivism: The European Phenomenon." *Studio International* 171, no. 876 (April 1966): 140–47.

Hill, Anthony. "Editor's Forward." In *Data: Directions in Art, Theory and Aesthetics*, edited by Anthony Hill, 5–6. London: Faber & Faber, 1968.

Hill, Anthony. "Max Bill: The Search for the Unity of the Plastic Arts in Contemporary Life." *Typographica* 7 (1953): 21–28.

Hill, Anthony. "Programme. Paragram. Structure." In *Data: Directions in Art, Theory and Aesthetics*, edited by Anthony Hill, 251–69. London: Faber & Faber, 1968.

Hitchcock, Henry-Russell. "The Architecture of Bureaucracy and the Architecture of Genius." *Architectural Review* 101, no. 601 (January 1947): 3–6.

Hopper, Ken, and Will Hopper. "Dan McCallum Creates the Multidivisional Corporation." In *The Puritan Gift: Triumph, Collapse and Revival of an American Dream*, 66–73. London: Tauris, 2007.

Iggers, Georg G. *Historiography in the Twentieth Century: From Scientific Objectivity to the Postmodern Challenge*. Hanover: Wesleyan University Press, 1997.

James, Alison. *Constraining Chance: Georges Perec and the Oulipo*.

Evanston: Northwestern University Press, 2009.

Jameson, Fredric. *The Prison-House of Language: A Critical Account of Structuralism and Russian Formalism*. Princeton: Princeton University Press, 1972.

Jencks, Charles. *The Language of Post-Modern Architecture*. New York: Rizzoli, 1977.

Jobse, Jonneke. *De Stijl Continued: The Journal Structure (1958–1964); An Artists' Debate*. Rotterdam: 010 Publishers, 2005.

Kovacs, Istvan. "Totality through Light: The Work of Laszlo Moholy-Nagy." *Form* 6 (December 1967): 14–19.

Kramer, Hilton. "Mondrian & Mysticism: 'My Long Search Is Over'." *New Criterion* 14 (September 1995): 4–14.

Krauss, Rosalind. "About October." *October* 1 (1976): 3.

Krauss, Rosalind. "Sculpture in the Expanded Field." *October* 8 (1979): 30–44.

Kubo, Michael. "The Anxiety of Anonymity: Bureaucracy and Genius in Late Modern Architecture Industry." In *New Constellations/New Ecologies, Proceedings of the 101st Annual Meeting of the ACSA*, 810–17. Washington D.C. ACSA, 2013.

Kuhn, Thomas. *The Structure of Scientific Revolutions*. Chicago: University of Chicago Press, 1962.

Ladkin, Sam, and Robin Purves. "An Introduction." *Chicago Review* 53, no. 1 (2007): 6–13.

Lassus, Bernard. "Environments and Total Landscape." *Form* 5 (September 1967): 13–15.

Le Corbusier. "The Quarrel with Realism: The Destiny of Painting." In *Circle: International Survey of Constructive Art*, edited by Leslie Martin, Ben Nicholson, and Naum Gabo, 67–74. London: Faber & Faber, 1937.

Lévi-Strauss, Claude. "The Structural Study of Myth." *Journal of American Folklore* 68, no. 270 (1955): 428–44.

Light, Jennifer S. "When Computers Were Women." *Technology and Culture* 40, no. 3 (1999): 455–83.

Lobsinger, Mary Louise. "Two Cambridges: Models, Methods, Systems, and Expertise." In *A Second Modernism: MIT, Architecture, and the "Techno-Social" Moment*, edited by Arindam Dutta, 652–85. Cambridge, MA: MIT Press, 2013.

Mahoney, Michael S. "The History of Computing in the History of Technology." *Annals of the History of Computing* 10, no. 2 (June 1988): 113–25.

Malina, Frank J. "Aims and Scope of Leonardo." *Leonardo* 1, no. 1 (January 1968): 1–2.

Manovich, Lev. *Software Takes Command*. New York: Bloomsbury Academic, 2013.

March, Lionel. "Introduction: The Logic of Design and the Question of Value." In *The Architecture of Form*, edited by Lionel March, 1–40. Cambridge: Cambridge University Press, 1976.

March, Lionel, Marcial Echenique, and Peter Dickens. "Models of Environment: Polemic for a Structural Revolution." *Architectural Design* 41 (May 1971): 275.

March, Lionel, and Philip Steadman. *The Geometry of Environment: An Introduction to Spatial Organization in Design*. London: RIBA, 1971.

Martin, Leslie. "Introduction." In *Circle: Constructive Art in Britain 1934–40*, edited by Jeremy Lewison, 5–6. Lavenham: Lavenham Press, 1982.

Martin, Leslie. "The State of Transition." In *Circle: International Survey of Constructive Art*, edited by Leslie Martin, Ben Nicholson, and Naum Gabo, 215–19. London: Faber & Faber, 1937.

Martin, Leslie, Ben Nicholson, and Naum Gabo, eds. *Circle: International Survey of Constructive Art*. London: Faber & Faber, 1937.

Meadows, Dennis, William Behrens III, Donella Meadows, Roger Naill, Jorgen Randers, and Erich Zahn. *Dynamics of Growth in a Finite World*. Cambridge, MA: Wright-Allen, 1974.

Meadows, Donella, Dennis Meadows, Jorgen Randers, and William W. Behrens III. *The Limits to Growth: A Report for the Club of Rome's Project on the Predicament of Mankind*. New York: Universe Books, 1972.

Mellor, David. *The Sixties Art Scene in London*. London: Phaidon, 1993.

Meltzer, Eve. *Systems We Have Loved: Conceptual Art, Affect, and the Antihumanist Turn*. Chicago: University of Chicago Press, 2013.

Merquior, J.G. *From Prague to Paris: A Critique of Structuralist and Post-Structuralist Thought*. London: Verso, 1986.

Miller, George. "The Magical Number Seven plus or Minus Two: Some Limits on Our Capacity for Processing Information." *Psychological Review* 101, no. 2 (1955): 343–52.

Mitchell, William J., Robin S. Liggett, and Thomas Kvan. *The Art of Computer Graphics Programming: A Structured Introduction for Architects and Designers*. New York: Van Nostrand Reinhold, 1987.

Mondrian, Piet. "Plastic Art and Pure Plastic Art (Figurative Art and Non-Figurative Art)." In *Circle: International Survey of Constructive Art*, edited by Leslie Martin, Ben Nicholson, and Naum Gabo, 41–56. London: Faber & Faber, 1937.

Monoskop. "Avant-Garde and Modernist Magazines," August 2014. http://monoskop.org/Avant-garde_and_modernist_magazines.

Montgomery, David. *The Fall of the House of Labor: The Workplace, the State, and American Labor Activism, 1865–1925*. Cambridge: Cambridge University Press, 1987.

Moreno, Joaquim. "Interview with Philip Steadman." In *Clip, Stamp, Fold: The Radical Architecture of Little Magazines, 196X to 197X*, edited by Beatriz Colomina, 507–9. Barcelona: Actar, 2011.

Moreno, Joaquim. "Interview with Stephen Bann." In *Clip, Stamp, Fold: The Radical Architecture of Little Magazines, 196X to 197X*, edited by Beatriz Colomina, 223–24. Barcelona: Actar, 2011.

Mosko, Mark S. "The Canonic Formula of Myth and Nonmyth." *American Ethnologist* 18, no. 1 (February 1991): 126–51.

Mumford, Lewis. "The Death of the Monument." In *Circle: International Survey of Constructive Art*, edited by Leslie Martin, Ben Nicholson, and Naum Gabo, 263–70. London: Faber & Faber, 1937.

Ngai, Sianne. "Merely Interesting." *Critical Inquiry* 34, no. 4 (2008): 777–817.

Nicholson, Ben. "Quotations." In *Circle: International Survey of Constructive Art*, edited by Leslie Martin, Ben Nicholson, and Naum Gabo, 75. London: Faber & Faber, 1937.

Nietzsche, Friedrich. *On the Advantage and Disadvantage of History for Life*. Translated by Peter Preuss. Indianapolis: Hackett, 1980.

Nieuwenhuys, Constant. "About the Meaning of Construction." In *Data: Directions in Art, Theory and Aesthetics*, edited by Anthony Hill, 175–79. London: Faber & Faber, 1968.

Osman, Michael. *Modernism's Visible Hand: Architecture and Regulation in America*. Minneapolis: University of Minnesota Press, 2018.

Overy, Paul, ed. *Mary Martin and Kenneth Martin: An Arts Council Touring Exhibition 1970–71*. London: Arts Council, 1970.

Pai, Hyungmin. *The Portfolio and the Diagram: Architecture, Discourse, and Modernity in America*. Cambridge, MA: MIT Press, 2002.

Perrault, Claude. *Ordonnance des cinq especes de colonnes selon* la methode des anciens. Paris: Jean Baptiste Coignard, 1683.

Pevsner, Nikolaus. "Report of a Debate on the Motion 'That Systems of Proportion Make Good Design Easier and Bad Design More Difficult'." *Journal of the Royal Institute of British Architects* 64, no. 11 (September 1957): 456–63.

Picon, Antoine. "Digital Technology and Architecture: Towards a Symmetrical Approach." *TAD* 6, no. 1 (2022): 10–14.

Picon, Antoine. "The Ghost of Architecture: The Project and Its Codification." *Perspecta* 35 (2004): 8–19.

Plato, Jan von. *The Great Formal Machinery Works: Theories of Deduction and Computation at the Origins of the Digital Age*. Princeton: Princeton University Press, 2017.

Rancière, Jacques. *Aisthesis: Scenes from the Aesthetic Regime of Art*. New York: Verso, 2011.

Reddy, William M. *The Navigation of Feeling: A Framework for the History of Emotions*. Cambridge: Cambridge University Press, 2001.

Richards, J.M. "The Condition of Architecture and the Principle of Anonymity." In *Circle: International Survey of Constructive Art*, edited by Leslie Martin, Ben Nicholson, and Naum Gabo, 184–89. London: Faber & Faber, 1937.

Rickey, George. *Constructivism: Origins and Evolution*. New York: Braziller, 1995.

Rosenberg, Daniel. "Data before the Fact." In *Raw Data Is an Oxymoron*, edited by Lisa Gitelman, 15–40. Cambridge, MA: MIT Press, 2013.

Rowe, Colin. "The Mathematics of the Ideal Villa: Palladio and Le Corbusier Compared." *Architectural Review* 101 (March 1947): 101–4.

Schwitters, Kurt. "Logically Consistent Poetry." *Form* 2 (September 1966): 28.

Sharr, Adam. *Demolishing Whitehall: Leslie Martin, Harold Wilson and the Architecture of White Heat*. Farnham, UK: Ashgate, 2013.

Sheppard, Robert. *The Poetry of Saying: British Poetry and Its Discontents, 1950–2000*. Liverpool: Liverpool University Press, 2005.

Skrebowski, Luke. "All Systems Go: Recovering Hans Haacke's Systems Art." *Grey Room* 30 (2008): 54–83.

Sperber, Dan. *On Anthropological Knowledge*. Cambridge: Cambridge University Press, 1985.

Steadman, Philip. "Colour Music." In *Kinetic Art: Four Essays*, edited by Stephen Bann, Reg Gadney, Frank Popper, and Philip Steadman, 16–25. St. Albans: Motion Books, 1966.

Steadman, Philip. "Research in Architecture and Urban Studies at Cambridge in the 1960s and 1970s: What Really Happened." *Journal of Architecture* 21, no. 2 (February 2016): 291–306.

Strauss, Claudia, and Naomi Quinn. *A Cognitive Theory of Cultural Meaning*. Cambridge: Cambridge University Press, 1997.

Sturrock, John. *Structuralism and Since: From Lévi Strauss to Derrida*. Oxford: Oxford University Press, 1979.

Summerson, John. "Architecture: A Changing Profession." *The Listener* 536 (April 1939): 830–32.

Summerson, John. "Bread & Butter and Architecture." *Horizon* vi (October 1942): 233–43.

Summerson, John. "Building Boom – I." *The Listener* 468 (December 1937): 1418–20.

Summerson, John. "Introduction." In *Modern Architecture in Britain*, edited by Trevor Dannatt, 11–28. London: Batsford, 1959.

Summerson, John. "London Re-Grouped." *The Listener* 755 (July 1943): 16.

Summerson, John. "The Case for a Theory of Modern Architecture." *Journal of the Royal Institute of British Architects* 64, no. 8 (June 1957): 307–10.

BIBLIOGRAPHY

Summerson, John. *The Classical Language of Architecture*. London: Methuen & Co, 1963.

Summerson, John. "TVA: Adventure in Planning." *The Listener* 774 (November 1943): 558.

Tschichold, Jan. "The New Typography." In *Circle: International Survey of Constructive Art*, edited by Leslie Martin, Ben Nicholson, and Naum Gabo, 249–55. London: Faber & Faber, 1937.

Turing, Alan. "On Computable Numbers, with an Application to the Entscheidungsproblem." *Proceedings of the London Mathematical Society 42*, no. 1 (1937): 230–65.

Upitis, Alise. "Nature Normative: The Design Methods Movement, 1944–1967." PhD thesis. Massachusetts Institute of Technology, 2008.

Uspenskii, V.A. "Algorithms, Theory of." In *Encyclopedia of Mathematics*. Berlin: Springer, 2002. http://encyclopediaofmath.org/index.php?title=Algorithms,_theory_of&oldid=45081.

Vantongerloo, Georges. "To Perceive / Universal-Existence? / Conception of Space 1 / Conception of Space 2." In *Data: Directions in Art, Theory and Aesthetics*, edited by Anthony Hill, 22–40. London: Faber & Faber, 1968.

Vardouli, Theodora. *Graph Vision: Digital Architecture's Skeletons*. Forthcoming. Cambridge, MA: MIT Press, 2024.

Vidler, Anthony. *Histories of the Immediate Present: Constructing Architectural Modernism*. Cambridge, MA: MIT Press, 2008.

Weaver, Mike. "Concrete and Kinetic: The Poem as Functional Object." *Image*, Special issue, *Kinetic Art: Concrete Poetry* 1964, 14–15.

Weaver, Mike. "Concrete Poetry." *Lugano Review* 1, no. 5 (1966): 100–125.

Wickersham, Jay. "Learning from Burnham: The Origins of American Architectural Practice." *Harvard Design Magazine* 32 (2010): 18–27.

Wigley, Mark. "Paper, Scissors, Blur." In *The Activist Drawing: Retracing Situationist Architectures from Constant's New Babylon to Beyond*, 27–56. Cambridge, MA: MIT Press, 1998.

Williams, Alena. "Movement in Vision: Cinema, Aesthetics, and Modern German Culture, 1918–1933." PhD thesis. Columbia University, 2014.

Wilson, Christopher. "Reputations: Richard Hollis." *Eye* 15, no. 59 (2006): 26–35.

Witt, Emily. "That Room in Cambridge." *n+1* 11 (2011): 73–98.

Zegher, Catherine de, and Mark Wigley, eds. *The Activist Drawing: Retracing Situationist Architectures from Constant's New Babylon to Beyond*. Cambridge, MA: MIT Press, 2001.

IMAGE CREDITS

1. Illustration by James Gardner
2. © The Museum of Modern Art / Licensed by SCALA / Art Resource, NY
3. © Constant / Fondation Constant c/o SODART, Canada / PRO LITTERIS, Zurich 2023
4. Photograph by Ernst Scheidegger © 2023 Stiftung Ernst Scheidegger-Archiv, Zurich
5. Harvard Art Museums / Busch-Reisinger Museum, Gift of Sibyl Moholy-Nagy. Photograph © President and Fellows of Harvard College, BR56.5
6. © F.L.C / ADAGP, Paris / Artists Rights Society (ARS), New York 2023
8. Zentrum Paul Klee, Bern, Bildarchiv
9. Photograph: Tate
10. © Angela Verren Taunt. All rights reserved, DACS, London / ARS, NY 2022. Photograph: Tate
12. © CNAC/MNAM, Dist. RMN-Grand Palais / Art Resource, NY
15. © 1985 Massachusetts Institute of Technology. All rights reserved
17. © F.L.C / ADAGP, Paris / Artists Rights Society (ARS), New York 2023
18. The Architectural Archives, University of Pennsylvania, by the gift of Robert Venturi and Denise Scott Brown
19. Courtesy Philip Steadman
21. Photograph: Graham Keen
22. Harvard Art Museums / Busch-Reisinger Museum, Gift of the artist. © Artists Rights Society (ARS), New York / VG Bild-Kunst, Bonn. Photograph © President and Fellows of Harvard College, BR48.97
23. Courtesy Philip Steadman
24. Courtesy Philip Steadman
26. Courtesy Philip Steadman
27. Courtesy Philip Steadman
30. Courtesy Bauhaus-Archiv Berlin
33. Courtesy of Albert Kahn Associates, Inc.
37. Courtesy HOK
40. Courtesy Charles Babbage Institute
42. Peter Eisenman fonds, Canadian Centre for Architecture
43. Courtesy Philip Steadman
44. Courtesy Philip Steadman
45. Courtesy Dennis Meadows

ACKNOWLEDGMENTS

I would like to thank Antoine Picon, K. Michael Hays, Catherine Ingraham, and Molly Wright Steenson for their generous dialogue as I researched and wrote this book. Picon's work in particular provided the intellectual context that made my own scholarship possible. Michael Meredith and Sanford Kwinter enlivened my thinking about art. Zeynep Çelik Alexander, John May, and Bernard Siegert directed me toward technics. Preston Scott Cohen insisted on the virtue of constraints. Theodora Vardouli and Daniel Cardoso Llach were insightful interlocutors. Philip Steadman and Stephen Bann provided invaluable comments on certain chapters. Phillip Thurtle and Jennifer Dee encouraged me on this path of inquiry ages ago. And to family—Merle Allen, Kathy Allen, Erica Kim, Leon Allen-Kim, and Elias Allen-Kim—I owe gratitude that goes beyond words. I dedicate this book to Elias and Leon.

gta edition is a peer-reviewed series of short monographs and edited volumes that take a fresh and provocative look at seemingly well-known aspects of architectural history to engage with contemporary historiography and the production of theory in architecture.

The infrastructure for this hybrid format, which technically and graphically combines the production of printed books with an online, open-access version, was developed collaboratively between gta Verlag and intercom Verlag.

gta-edition.ch

Series concept
Moritz Gleich, Niki Rhyner, Max Stadler

Graphic concept and design
Reinhard Schmidt, Nadine Wüthrich

Development
Urs Hofer

Content management and copyediting
Jennifer Bartmess

Proofreading
Thomas Skelton-Robinson

Printing
TBS, La Buona Stampa SA, Switzerland

Binding
Bubu AG, Switzerland

Typeface
ABC Diatype

Paper
Invercote G FSC 200 g/m²
Munken Print White 1.5 FSC 100 g/m²

Cover image
Stephen Flanders, DYNAMO flow diagram of the World3 model, 1972
Courtesy Dennis Meadows© 2025

© 2025, 2nd printing
gta Verlag, ETH Zurich
Institute for the History and Theory of Architecture
Department of Architecture
Stefano-Franscini-Platz 5
8093 Zurich, Switzerland
www.verlag.gta.arch.ethz.ch
verlag@gta.arch.ethz.ch

© Texts: by the authors
© Illustrations: by the image authors and their legal successors; for copyrights, see image credits

Every reasonable attempt has been made by the author and the publisher to identify owners of copyrights. Should any errors or omissions have occurred, please notify us.

Creative Commons CC BY-NC-ND

Responsible person according to EU regulation 2023/988
GVA Gemeinsame Verlagsauslieferung Göttingen GmbH & Co. KG
Postfach 2021
37010 Göttingen, Germany
info@gva-verlage.de
+49 (0)551 38 42 00-0

ISSN (print) 2813-2505
ISSN (PDF) 2813-2513
ISBN (print) 978-3-85676-445-6
ISBN (PDF) 978-3-85676-461-6
DOI https://doi.org/10.54872/gta/4616